Women on the Italian Literary Scene

Women on the Italian Literary Scene: A Panorama

by
Alba della Fazia Amoia

The Whitston Publishing Company
Troy, New York
1992

For my two sisters
and
Angela Cavalcanti

Contents

Chronology

1846	Birth of Neera in Milan and of Marchesa Colombi in Novara.
1856	Matilde Serao born in Patras, Greece.
1868	Annie Vivanti born in London.
1870	Ada Negri born in Lodi.
1871	Grazia Deledda born in Sardinia.
1876	Sibilla Aleramo born in Alessandria.
1877	*Un romanzo*, Neera's first published novel.
1878	Marchesa Colombi's *In risaia* published.
1881	Italian realism (*verismo*) and regionalism prevail on the literary scene.
1883	*Cuore infermo*, Matilde Serao's first published novel.
1887	Maria Messina born in Sicily.
1890	Grazia Deledda publishes her first novel, *Stella d'Oriente*, under the pseudonym Ilia di Saint-Ismael.
1891	*Marion, artista di caffé concerto*, Annie Vivanti's first published novel.
1895	Anna Banti born in Florence.
1896	Gianna Manzini born in Pistoia.
1900	Fausta Cialente born in Cagliari.
1902	Maria Bellonci born in Rome.
1906	*Una donna*, Sibilla Aleramo's first published novel.
1909	Lalla Romano born in Demonte (Cuneo).
1911	Alba de Céspedes born in Rome. Publication of Annie Vivanti's novel *I divoratori* (first published in London in 1910 as *The Devourers*).
1912	Elsa Morante born in Rome.
1913	Livia De Stefani born in Sicily.

1914	Anna Maria Ortese born in Rome.
1916	Natalia Ginzburg born in Palermo.
1918	Death of Neera.
1920	Death of Marchesa Colombi.
1921	Publication of Ada Negri's only novel, *Stella mattutina*.
	Maria Messina's *La casa nel vicolo* published.
1922	Beginning of 18-year fascist regime in Italy.
1926	Nobel Prize for Literature awarded to Grazia Deledda.
	Founding of Bagutta Prize, oldest of Italy's literary prizes.
1927	Death of Matilde Serao.
1928	*Tempo innamorato*, Gianna Manzini's first published novel.
	Birth of Francesca Sanvitale in Milan.
1929	Founding of Viareggio Prize.
1930	Birth of Oriana Fallaci in Florence.
1931	Ada Negri wins first Mussolini Prize for literature.
	Rosetta Loy born in Rome.
1935	Gianna Manzini receives prize of encouragement from Royal Academy of Italy (inaugurated in 1929).
1936	Death of Grazia Deledda.
	Birth of Dacia Maraini in Florence.
1937	*Cosima*, Grazia Deledda's autobiographical novel, published posthumously.
	Itinerario di Paolina, Anna Banti's first published novel.
	Fascist anti-Semitic laws passed in Italy.
1938	*Nessuno torna indietro*, Alba de Céspedes's first published novel, banned by the fascist government in 1940.
1939	Maria Bellonci's *Lucrezia Borgia* published and awarded Viareggio Prize.
1940	Ada Negri is first woman to become member of Accademia d'Italia.
1941	Italian postwar neorealism begins to define itself.
	Elsa Morante marries novelist Alberto Moravia (the couple becomes estranged in 1963).
1942-1944	Many Italian women, some of them writers (e.g. Natalia Ginzburg, Oriana Fallaci, Carla Voltolina, Camilla Ravera, Marina Jarre, Iris Origo, Renata

	Viganò, Marina Sereni), active in the antifascist resistance movement during World War II.
1942	*La strada che va in città*, Natalia Ginzburg's first published novel.
	Death of Annie Vivanti, abandoned and in misery, in Torino.
1943	A group of women (Ada Gobetti, Rina Picolato, Lina Merlin, Elena Dreher, etc.) belonging to the antifascist parties found women's "defense groups" in Piedmont and Lombardy.
1944	Three months after the liberation of Italy, the Unione Donne Italiane (UDI) officially constituted in Rome on 15 September.
	Death of Maria Messina.
1945	Italian women gain the vote.
	Neorealism firmly established in Italian literature and cinema.
	Death of Ada Negri.
	Gianna Manzini's *Lettera all'editore* published.
1947	Maria Bellonci and others found the Strega Prize.
	Anna Banti's *Artemisia* published.
1948	*Menzogna e sortilegio*, Elsa Morante's first published novel, awarded Viareggio Prize.
1950	First law passed for protection of working mothers.
1952	Natalia Ginzburg's *Tutti i nostri ieri* and Alba de Céspedes's *Quaderno proibito* published.
1953	Anna Maria Ortese's *Il mare non bagna Napoli* awarded Viareggio Prize.
	La vigna delle uve nere, Livia de Stefani's first published novel.
1956	Gianna Manzini's *La sparviera* awarded Viareggio Prize.
1957	Elsa Morante's *L'isola di Arturo* published, and subsequently (1966) awarded Strega Prize.
	Law passed granting "equal rights for equal work."
1960	Death of Sibilla Aleramo.
1962	Founding of Campiello Prize.
	La vacanza, Dacia Maraini's first published novel.
	By law, "paternal" authority replaced by "parental" authority within the family.
1963	Natalia Ginzburg's *Lessico famigliare* awarded Strega Prize.

Elsa Morante's *Lo scialle andaluso,* a collection of twelve stories, published in book form.

Law gives parents parity of decisive powers in certain family, business and residence matters.

Law grants access by women to all public offices and possibility for full career in public administration.

1965   Anna Maria Ortese's most important novel, *L'iguana,* published.

1966   Elsa Morante's *L'isola di Arturo,* published in 1957, awarded Strega Prize.

1967   *Poveri e semplici,* by Anna Maria Ortese, published.

1968   Elsa Morante's *Il mondo salvato dai ragazzini,* a collection of poetry, published and highly acclaimed. (Awarded Zafferana Prize.)

Students' and workers' "revolutions" give impetus to the feminist emancipatory movements that proliferate in the 1970s.

1969   Lalla Romano's *Le parole tra noi leggere* awarded Strega Prize.

1970   Divorce established in Italy.

1971   Gianna Manzini's *Ritratto in piedi* awarded Campiello Prize.

Law passed for subsidy by national government of nursery schools.

Second law passed for protection of working mothers.

1972   *Il cuore borghese,* Francesca Sanvitale's first published novel.

1973   Anna Banti's *La camicia bruciata* and Gianna Manzini's *Sulla soglia* published.

Natalia Ginzburg's *La famiglia Manzoni* awarded Bagutta Prize.

Protective legislation passed for women in cottage industries.

1974   Elsa Morante's *La Storia* published.

Rosetta Loy's first novel, *La bicicletta,* awarded Viareggio Prize.

Popular referendum results in decisive defeat of papal and Christian-Democrat attempts to annul divorce law.

Death of Gianna Manzini.

1975	World Conference for International Women's Year and Declaration of Mexico City has significant repercussion in Italy.
1976	Fausta Cialente's *Le quattro ragazze Wieselberger* awarded Strega Prize.
1978	Voluntary interruption of pregnancy legalized, but full application of law still lacking today.
1979	Oriana Fallaci's *Un uomo* published.
1980	Francesca Sanvitale's *Madre e figlia* published.
1981	Fabrizia Ramondino's *Althénopis* published.
1982	Elsa Morante's last novel, *Aracoeli*, published.
1983	Suicide attempt by Elsa Morante.
1985	Death of Elsa Morante and Anna Banti. Publication of Maria Bellonci's last historical novel, *Rinascimento privato*. Natalia Ginzburg wins Pirandello literary prize.
1986	Death of Maria Bellonci.
1987	"Prix théâtre italien contemporain" awarded to Natalia Ginzburg and Italo Svevo. Rita Levi Montalcini, 1986 Nobel Prize winner for Medicine, publishes *Elogio dell'imperfezione*.
1988	Rosetta Loy wins both the Campiello and the Viareggio prizes for her novel, *Le strade di polvere*, published in 1987.
1989	Congress of Italian housewives decides to form a political party in 1992.
1990	Dacia Maraini's *La lunga vita di Marianna Ucrìa* awarded Campiello Prize. Luisa Adorno wins Viareggio Prize for her autobiographical novel, *Arco di luminara*. Bagutta Prize awarded to Fleur Jaeggy for her novel, *I beati anni del castigo*.
1991	Death of Natalia Ginzburg. Isabella Bossi Fedrigotti's *Di buona famiglia* awarded the Campiello Prize. Grazia Livi wins the Viareggio Prize for her book of essays, *Le lettere del mio nome*.

Preface

Nobel Prize-winner Rita Levi Montalcini,[1] in her stunning autobiography entitled *Elogio dell'imperfezione* (In praise of imperfection, 1987), concludes that human activities are tempered by educational rather than genetic factors. Language, she claims, humankind's greatest privilege, may either open up infinite horizons of thought or plunge it into the depths of obscurantism. Her summing up of the cognitive, constructive, and destructive capacities of human thought may be taken as the point of departure for this aperçu of nineteenth- and twentieth-century Italian women writers and their modes of expression.

The double aim of such a broad panorama is to identify the writers and give the reader a quicker sense of their role in carrying the human race forward towards what the French philosopher, Teilhard de Chardin, has called the "crown of the noosphere"—that is, the highest representation of the "thinking layer" of the human mind during the course of evolutionary development.[2] For Teilhard de Chardin, as for Levi Montalcini, thought evolves and progresses, ultimately to reach a final unity—the "All," or the collective superconsciousness.

Very consciously, women writers in Italy, as elsewhere, are now taking an active part in minimizing the importance of their biological function in an effort to concentrate on the higher level of philosophical thought. They are more interested in improving the level of general thinking than in militating for women's rights or theorizing total separation from the other sex. They seek to define thought and language in the feminine, but their thinking does not allow them to preclude all of humanity's reaching the "All," which must amalgamate male and female minds.

Groups of erudite women have formed in Italy: in Milan at the Libreria delle Donne and the Hypatia circle (named after the first feminist victim, the philosopher murdered by a Christian mob in Alexandria in 415); in Rome at the historical Virginia Woolf center. In Bologna, outstanding women have grouped around the Orlando Women's Association, in Naples around the review *Transizione*, while in Brescia a university for women has been created. Perhaps the best-known concentration of Italian women intellectuals may be found in Verona's Diotima group, named after the priestess evoked by Socrates in Plato's *Symposium*. The Diotima group of distinguished thinkers champion a philosophical concept of non-neutral *"differenza sessuale*," inspired by the writings of Luce Irigaray and developed by the Milanese Libreria della Donne group.

Italy's clusters of women writers and thinkers are beginning to incarnate a feminine authority, which gradually is making itself felt in the professional and institutional worlds. Their works, or the women themselves through their life style, spirit of observation, refinement of humor, or distinctive literary style, are joining the ranks of humankind's elite, using the written word to achieve the best possible literary and philosophical expression of certain truths.

Elsa Morante is perhaps the Italian woman writer who has best told her readers that humanity, even though attached to the past, is slowly evolving to a higher form of organic unity. It is she who has sustained with the most conviction that, through books and abstract thought, the world must change. Her very definition of a novel as a "poetic work" equates poet and novelist. For her, nature is the perfect reality, truer than any historic reality, so that the more woman becomes woman, the more she will feel herself moving toward the endless and indestructible "new reality" that Morante contemplated. In her introductory note to her book of poetry, *Il mondo salvato dai ragazzini* (The world saved by little children), Morante wonders about the nature of reality in this scientific age of unreal and unnatural horrors, declaring that "no poet, today, can ignore the desperate . . . question of other living beings. More than ever, the reasons for [the poet's] presence in the world is to look for an answer for himself and for others."[3] The anguish of the individual—male or female—has become the anguish of the collective. No element moves or grows unaccompanied. If there are doors leading to a better reality, they will open up only if all humanity pushes together.

Compared with Anglo-Saxon societies, Mediterranean Italy was late in emancipating its women, and even later in discovering their intellectual autonomy. Grazia Deledda, in the fervent belief that only by "drawing close to masterpieces can we attempt to better ourselves a bit,"[4] broke loose from her mother's moral fettering and her backward townspeople's cries of "scandal!" at her choice of career, and moved forward and higher to become the Nobel Prize winner for Literature in 1926.

Only relatively recently have Italian women been given the freedom to judge their own existence as well as that of men, to criticize their role in society, externalize their unconscious needs, and display their feminine creativity. Having cast off the blinkers of dependence on the male, and submissive maternity, they now probe their inner depths to discern what lies under the skin of the graceful female form. Having adjusted to new perspectives in disposing of themselves and their talents, women writers and thinkers can now strive to reach the "crown of the noosphere" with the expectation of finding harmony with both themselves and the rest of society. What importance have authors of the ilk of Grazia Deledda and Elsa Morante if not, through their consciousness, illumination, and assertion of authority, to help other women emerge from their anonymity through education and imitation? The importance of reading the works of women authors is better to recognize oneself in them—the man will recognize his *anima*, the woman her *animus*—and better to understand humankind's combinative destiny.

The world of feminine literature is just discovering its own evolution. Up to the end of the 1960s, Italian women authors perhaps did not see themselves as protagonists of an evolution in course; now, women's writings form a new collective thought[5]—a symbolic representation of humanity's forward movement. Today, when old myths about the earth's creators and explorers seem to be weakening their grip on the human imagination, new myths are needed. Zeus's cosmogonic labors and Ulysses's daring voyages have dwindled in the mind perched at the edge of the solar system. Yet how difficult it is to escape conventional thinking patterns. The written word alone helps to free one's mental faculties and steer the intellect in its infinite quests. Perhaps Italy's future women writers will be among those whispering into the ears of twenty-first-century children that *they* represent the heroic age of mankind and that *their* exploits are destined to be the new myths. But whatever evolution and new world view the next century brings, it will still be the *word* that will broach "the troubles of the brain."

I am indebted to the authors or editors of my heavily-thumbed copies of *Contemporary Women Writers in Italy. A Modern Renaissance* (Professor Santo L. Aricò); *Quel mondo dei guanti e delle stoffe . . .* (Paola Blelloch); *Scritture, scrittrici* (Maria Rosa Cutrufelli); *L'ora di Lilith* (Neria De Giovanni); *La voce che è in lei. Antologia della narrativa femminile tra '800 e '900* (Giuliana Morandini); and *Tabù e coscienza* (Anna Noz-zoli)—all of which have helped to keep this survey on its course. Responsibility for errors and other shortcomings must, of course, remain with me, and if some Italian women novelists whose voices deserve to be heard have inadvertently been omitted, the oversight is mine. No poets are included in this volume.

The titles of the works of the women writers included in this book are given in both Italian and English at the first mention in the text. All translations of quotations are my own unless otherwise noted.

I wish to express my thanks to Dr. Umberto Righetti for his valuable socio-political insights into the twentieth-century Italian scene. An expression of appreciation is due also to Professor Bettina L. Knapp; to Elisabetta Alvi and the library staff of Radio Televisione Italiana (RAI); to Maria-Teresa Barbieri; and to the knowledgeable personnel of the women's bookshop "Al Tempo Ritrovato" in Rome.

Rome, 1991   Alba della Fazia Amoia

Chapter One

Introduction

A.   The "Feminine" in Italian Literature

What forms the corpus of "feminist" and "neofeminist" literature can easily be identified (see Chapter Six, below). But what constitutes strictly "feminine" writing has not yet been determined. The debate that began in the 1970s on the subject of the gender of language as a tool for literary description and interpretation is still unresolved. Rejecting the idea that there can be a "feminine language," and arguing against the formation of a separate category for women's writings, an increasing number of Italian authors sustain that any distinction between "*scrittori*" and "*scrittrici*" is purposeless, since writing transcends sex and there are no strictly feminine themes. (The word "*scrittore*" should, in fact, be used for all authors of creative, balanced, artistic literary works, although women who write as journalists, feminine ideologists, psychologists, and sociologists, might, perhaps, be referred to as "*scrittrici*."[1])

Wide support is accorded to Marguerite Duras's concept[2] that literature is an immense continent on which George Sand's works are not "feminine" any more than Marcel Proust's are "masculine." The works of these authors are simply literature, and as such they represent neutral sources of knowledge and pleasure. Yet neutrality is still challenged by many female thinkers and writers who sustain that the world looks very different indeed if it is described and interpreted by a man or by a woman.

No longer can one identify feminine literature with sentimentalism or "rosy" novels for adolescent girls. Nor can one continue to catalog as strictly feminine the themes of female sexuality, childbirth, abortion, lesbianism, and domesticity. If themes such as society's vengeance on women who transgress its moral code, the adulterous woman's rejection of hypocritical proprieties, and the sincerity of woman's love, could be classified as feminine, then one would have to affirm that Lev Tolstoi—at least in *Anna Karenina*—is a very great woman writer; and if such themes as the creation of an empire, the regulation of military discipline, and male homosexual love, are strictly male, then one would likewise have to assert that Marguerite Yourcenar—at least in *Hadrian's Memoirs*—is a great male writer.

The Italian feminine literary voice of the 1990s mingles with that of the male even though it is still seeking subjectively to find values and social measures different from neutral or masculine ones. This new voice constitutes the link between sociopolitical and cultural feminism. It is an effort to use to women's advantage the "*differenza sessuale*" by building a new culture around it, and by bringing richness, novelty, and plurality into the complexities of Italian society. Disagreements among women on the language issues of the 1970s now seem to be dissolving in favor of a more harmonious philosophical closeness.

Women writers have reached a point of literary selffulfillment, having demonstrated their genius in capturing the workings of the psyche, the sense of rhythmic and cyclical time, and the essence of the particular, the small, and the fragile. Disinclined to "copy,"[3] and intent on "making culture," they participate, interpret, and debate together with men but without ever renouncing their right to use feminine apparatus in filtering and transmuting contemporary cultural and literary elements.

A significant feminine presence in Italian literature dates from the end of the nineteenth century, when women were waging a bitter struggle to achieve emancipation. Before the turn of the century, creative Italian women were stymied in their artistic or literary endeavors. Looking still further back in time, one notes that even during the periods of poetic exaltation of the "gentle sex" (troubadour and Renaissance literature), there persisted in Italy restrictive religious concepts and traditions which repressed women's aspirations even on the simple level of their own *raison d'être*, much less that of personal creativity. (It must be recalled that at least up to the first millenium, representatives of the Roman Catholic Church had questioned whether a rational spirit should be attributed to the female.)

Material conditions further precluded women's entertaining of any foolish literary ambitions. Even those born into rich, noble, or powerful families did not escape a destiny of house chores. A few examples exist of Italian women's capacity for organizing cultural activities, but they must be sought among those fortunate enough to have contracted royal marriages abroad, such as Catherine and Marie de Medicis. Although a limited number of women poets distinguished themselves during the Renaissance, illiteracy was so widespread that in not a few cases Italian courtesans successful in creating what would be called today "literary salons" were incapable of reading or writing.

The presence of Spanish power in Italy curbed the political freedom of the Renaissance courts, causing women writers practically to disappear from the scene. Their presence again began to be felt discreetly in the religious movements of the Counter-Reformation. Throughout the eighteenth and nineteenth centuries, women's writings adhered quite strictly to the masculine *weltanschauung*.[4] Finally, with the gradual assertion of democratic ideals in the twentieth century, the way was paved in Italy for a radical change in the status of women writers and intellectuals.

Between the end of the nineteenth century and the beginning of the twentieth, women writers strove to create a model of a "new feminism" which would legitimize their role in the contemporary world.[5] Their early literary attempts—heartfelt but ingenuous—were descriptions of the suffering of women, especially in the countryside. Using a coarse, direct style, they delineated miserable, humble characters in a setting that combined gritty realism and an arcadian search for moral edification. Although well-intentioned, the authors of these works were still far from effectively denouncing women's socio-economic plight. What the writers succeeded in illustrating was the industrious, pastoral life which ideally could become an example for humanity of a pure and perfect existence. Early examples of this peasant populism will be found in the works of Caterina Percoto and Matilde Serao.

The most significant woman representative of the turn-of-the-century regional and realistic novel was Grazia Deledda who, after Giovanni Verga, was the outstanding writer of the school of *verismo*.[6] Just as Verga realistically describes the life of Sicily's peasants and fishermen, Deledda brings readers into contact with the psychology of Sardinia's primitive human beings against a backdrop of distinctive regional landscapes. Only during the years of World War I did Deledda intuit the changes taking place in world literature. Overstepping the confines of traditional verist canons, she began channeling her capacity for conjuring up visions of nature into a vaguely romantic and naturalistic preoccupation with the shabby realities of the poor. The new trend was to shift focus from the peasantry to the *"piccola borghesia"* (the lower middle class) and *"il popolino"* (the hoi polloi).

Two literary trends were evolving towards the end of the nineteenth century: one characterized by sentimentalism, eroticism, and decadence, the other concerned with women's sociopolitical problems. Italian women authors of the second trend, taking up the banner of feminine libertarianism, exposed the plight of the lower classes. Ada Negri, for example, accurately portrayed the sadness and loneliness of her feminine condition and voiced her rebellion against the victimization of females. Annie Vivanti, even though an antifeminist (see Chapter Six, below), clarified the reasons for women's feelings of alienation in an imbalanced society. But it is Sibilla Aleramo who occupies the most important position in the panorama of literary feminism in the early twentieth century. Her novel, *Una donna* (*A Woman*[7]), published in 1906 during a period of reformist socialism, is still today a text of fundamental importance.

World War I was the crucial period when the two literary trends combined, continuing up to the 1960s in the margins of the patriarchal mainstream of dominant literary currents. In vogue between the end of the 1930s and the 1960s was the historical novel or more or less fictionalized historical biography. For some authors, the genre served as a means of escape from fascist censorship, but many women writers succeeded in using apparently innocuous chronicles of the past in order to focus on contemporary issues. Concomitantly there was an upsurge of erudite art and literary criticism: this was the era of Bernard Berenson, Roberto Longhi, Emilio Cecchi, and Goffredo Bellonci, whose critiques still today condition the analyses and evaluations of art and literature. It is no coincidence that the two major women historical novelists, Anna Banti and Maria Bellonci (see Chapter Three, below), were married, respectively, to Longhi and Bellonci.

The problems of work and self-fulfillment which faced educated leftist women in the 1950s are exposed in Maria Luisa Aguirre D'Amico's *Come si può* (1986). The revolutionary eruptions of the late 1960s and the specifically subversive nature of the writings of the 1970s helped women to hasten the process of achieving parity with the male and acceding to Italy's social, political, and literary institutions. Why most Italian feminist writers belong to movements of the Left[8] may be explained in both historical and sociological terms. Elsewhere in Europe, as far back as the era of the Crusades, chatelaines, left alone to administer the family's activities, became aware of their potential to wield influence in their limited economic and cultural worlds. Their function was not only to inspire poetry and troubadours' songs but also to represent important interests in the feudal society of the time. Naturally, reference is made here to the ruling classes, for women belonging to the farming, artisan, and commercial classes lived in a state of total subjection; sometimes their value in the household was equated with that of a domestic animal.

Although few in number, European women of rank who had achieved emancipation emerged as literate, cultured figures constituting the earliest nucleus of independent women struggling to improve their status. For other humiliated and repressed women, they became almost a symbol of feminine potential. Even though this elite feminine group never acquired a position of hegemony, it did participate in the development of arts and letters and in the evolution of tastes and customs of their societies through their literary salons.

A similar feminine crusading spirit was not manifest in Italy, except perhaps briefly in Medicean Florence. While the rest of Europe was undergoing reformation, abortive Roman Catholic conservatism was forcing Galileo to recant and causing Giordano Bruno to be burned at the stake. Such obscurantism helped to retard the evolution of Italian women and dashed all hopes for any measure of emancipation or independence of thought.

Thus, the battle taken up by Italian women, as late as the twentieth century, was a total one, to vindicate social, cultural, economic, and political rights.[9] Socialism, especially in its typical reformist aspect, appealed to women militating for their liberation. Catholic political movements concerned themselves mainly with encouraging and protecting motherhood in order to swell their future ranks,[10] while anarchical groups stressed the problem of women's sexual liberation.[11] The Socialist party and the Socialist trade unions, on the other hand, best gave expression to women's demands for parity in the political, institutional, and economic fields, through the efforts of such strenuous leaders as Anna Kuliscioff, Maria Giudice, and Argentina Altobelli.

The leftist connotations of the Italian feminist movement were obscured during the fascist era, when women were reduced substantially to being "prolific mothers" and "rural house-wives." Women's writings of the period underwent significant improvement of style and structure—but not of content.

The end of World War II and the return of democracy to Italy saw a remarkable display of vitality and maturity in Italian narrative literature. Postwar neorealism (characterized as "magic realism" and best represented in this volume by Elsa Morante and Anna Maria Ortese) was rooted in nineteenth-century *verismo* but differed in that reality was not historically but lyrically evoked. Although the genre became petrified by the 1950s,[12] in the late 1980s there was a noticeable return to a fic-tionalized "heroic realism" of everyday life in Italian novels, po-etry, songs, films, and television programs, which has come to be referred to as "neo-neorealism."

The world of women's writings has been encapsulated in the genres of the realistic and regional novels, the historical and epistolary novels, and, above all, in "*letteratura della memoria*" (memory writing), a narrative vehicle that permits description of past experience through the double filter of time and imagina-tion. Recent studies of the autobiography have emphasized that imagination plays a substantial role in the genre and shares a number of primary features with fiction: "Autobiographies, as much as novels, depend on narration, provide explanations, and insist on the comprehensibility of life."[13] Talented Italian women authors writing in the genre have gone beyond the mere need to construct a reassuring identity for themselves by rein-venting their family histories. Some have succeeded in widen-ing their thematic concerns outside the scope of personal experi-ence in order to attack the social order. "*Letteratura della memoria*" is perhaps best represented in this volume by Gianna Manzini and Natalia Ginzburg (see Chapter Four, below). Manzini was to express life's sadness in a decadent style, while Ginzburg, in her neorealistic style, gives an ironic twist and a more positive turn to her protagonists' struggle against outra-geous destiny.

The place of the unrivaled Elsa Morante among writers of regional, historical, epistolary, and autobiographical novels at-tests to her uniqueness on the Italian literary scene. Her sharp sense of history and her musical juggling of words are matched by her adroitness in deception—the hallmark of her masterpiece, *Menzogna e sortilegio* (*House of Liars*,[14] see Chapter Four, below). Morante writes with melancholy, fantasy, and a dash of lunacy. For her, the world is warmth, perfume, and light, and the festive humorism that sometimes penetrates it lends support to her solemn flights of fancy. She writes of animals, jewelry, furniture, and cupboards in such a way that they become as alive as human beings. The reader cannot fail to savor her prose, absorbing every perfume and every flavor she pours into it. The dramatic opposition in Morante's oeuvre between the gloominess of *Menzogna e sortilegio* and the brightness of her novel which is considered a milestone in Italian literature, *L'isola di Arturo* (*Arturo's Island*), has been aptly commented for Italian television viewers by author Francesca Sanvitale, herself a master of dark and light contrasts.[15] Morante is undoubtedly the most successful and widely read woman author in modern Italian literature; her novels are surely those most likely to survive in the schemas of Italy's future literary panoramas.

Due mention will be made, in the last chapter of this volume, of numerous miscellaneous authors who, by force of personal conviction or through sheer audacity, have contributed to the literary scene and testified to changing values in Italian society. Oriana Fallaci, for example, in elaborating her themes of deep civil and political commitment, eminently succeeds in overcoming the limitations of her journalistic trade; Lidia Ravera, having survived confiscation of her first novel for its obscenity (which guaranteed its commercial success), is publishing frothy novels at a steady pace; Francesca Duranti has repeatedly captured the attention of literary prize juries for her revisitations in a modern key of "*letteratura della memoria*"; and a handful of debutants are quietly and self-possessedly stepping on to the platform of the Italian literary stage.

The subject of gender and genre in Italian feminist literature in the 1970s has been studied elsewhere.[16] Whether language can expose the oppression of women based on sexual difference, and produce changes in society, is still a subject of debate. Here the simple questions may be raised as to whether the genres chosen by Italian women writers have served as the most appropriate vehicles to express their rupture with society and change their relationship with the work world and family members; whether a distinguishable evolution of Italian tastes and culture is traceable in their works; whether they have lured the Italian woman from the traditional concepts of maternity, thereby raising her intellectual and professional sights; whether they have stirred both parents' and children's awareness of their mutual socio-politico-ecological responsibilities; and whether they have helped both men and women to discover that beyond family ties there are freely chosen bonds which are stronger than consanguinity. Most of these questions probably will be answered, however, only when perceptions of Italian women as a historical group have begun to crystallize. Here, one can simply look at the literary facet of this evolving group.

B.   The "Feminine" in Italian Literary Prizes

An increasing number of women writers have become literary prize winners over the past decades. Natalia Ginzburg rates third among writers who have captured the most of Italy's literary prizes, and Elsa Morante is ranked among the most meritorious in the forty-odd-year history of the Strega Prize. Others who have won the Strega Prize are Anna Maria Ortese, Lalla Romano, Maria Bellonci, and Fausta Cialente, while different prizes have been awarded to an ever-growing number of women authors for their poetry, essays, novels, or short story collections. (Important prize-winning titles will be indicated in the chapters below.)

Among the most prestigious of the many so-called "wheels of fortune" may be cited the Bagutta, the Viareggio, the Strega, and the Campiello prizes. The Bagutta, oldest of Italian literary prizes (distribution was interrupted during World War II but resumed in 1948), was founded on November 11, 1926, at the table of Milan's Bagutta restaurant, by a group of writer friends. The most recent awarding of the Bagutta Prize to a woman author was in 1990, when Fleur Jaeggy, a Swiss writer who lives in Milan and writes in Italian, received the distinction for her novel, *I beati anni del castigo* (The blessed years of punishment).

The Viareggio Prize was founded in 1929 by the writer Leonida Repaci and a group of intellectual friends, who conceived of a literary distinction quite different from the fruit of the Bagutta supper table coterie. The Viareggio is a "beach prize," sponsored by the many literary figures who live in that part of Tuscany known as Versilia. The prizes for the best novel, the best collection of essays, and for an author's first published work, are conferred in the gardens of Villa Borbone in Viareggio.

Unlike the other prizes, the Viareggio does not admit of "official" candidates. Final voting is by a jury of well-known personalities in the cultural world, usually of a specific political orientation, as demonstrated by the "special" nonliterary prizes awarded to Alexander Panagoulis in 1969 (see Oriana Fallaci's *Un uomo* [*A Man*] Chapter Seven, below); to Willy Brandt in 1989; and to the English historian of Marxism, Eric Hobsbawm, in 1991. Rosetta Loy won both the Viareggio and the Campiello prizes in 1988 for her novel, *Le strade di polvere* (Dusty roads, see Chapter Three, below). Natalia Ginzburg was one of the members of the Viareggio jury both in 1989, when Maria Corti's book of short stories, *Canto delle sirene* (Song of the sirens) and Paola Capriolo's novel, *Il nocchiero* (The helmsman), were originally in the running but were not among the finalists; and in 1990, when Luisa Adorno was awarded the prize for her autobiographical novel, *Arco di luminara* (Illuminated arch). Susanna Tamaro was among the finalists for the 1991 Viareggio Prize for her book of short stories, *Per voce sola* (Voice solo), which nevertheless won two lesser prizes, while Grazia Livi was awarded the prize for her essays, *Le lettere del mio nome*, for that year.

The Strega Prize, first launched in 1947, was the felicitous idea of Maria and Goffredo Bellonci, in whose salon known as *"Gli Amici della Domenica"* ("Sunday Friends"), even today famous literary figures cast their preliminary vote to choose five novels, further refining their selection until the awarding of the prize, which invariably takes place on a summer's evening in the splendid Renaissance gardens of Vignola's Villa Giulia in Rome. Here the same "Friends" (not without considerable loud backstage bickering) eventually cast their second ballots. The defect of the Strega Prize is that it is easily manipulated by the publishing industry, the judges being writers or persons connected with the various Italian publishing houses. Since the death of Maria Bellonci in 1986, the prize has been plagued by what has been called the "Premio Strega syndrome": violent clashes and personal improprieties among candidates, supporters, and jury, causing the Strega to be characterized as the most spiteful of all the Italian literary prizes. Clara Sereni's book of short stories, *Manicomio primavera* (Spring insane asylum) was among the finalists for the 1989 prize, while in 1990 three women authors were among the fourteen original candidates: Carla Cerati for her novel, *La cattiva figlia* (The bad daughter), Marina Jarre for the historical novel, *Ascanio e Margherita* (Ascanius and Margaret), and Giovanna Vizzari for *Medea*. In 1991, Gina Lagorio and Angela Bianchini were among the finalists for *Tra le mura stellate* (Within the star-shaped walls) and *Capo d'Europa* (Cape Europe), respectively.

The Campiello Prize, whose creation by the Industrial Union of Venice dates to 1962, is in essence the domain of the Mondadori publishers. Here, a "technical jury" first chooses fifteen novels, from which a second slate of five is drawn; these are then submitted to the judgment of a "popular jury" composed of three hundred unidentified readers belonging to different professional and social groups. Catering to average tastes, and perhaps lacking sufficient literary representativeness, the not too highly qualified popular jury chooses the one novel it deems most worthy of the prize. For the first time in the history of the Campiello, a woman was called to the honor of presiding over the awarding of the prize in 1989: Gae Aulenti, the Italian architect whose plans for the restructuring of the Paris railroad station into the present D'Orsay Museum gained her worldwide fame. Also a first occurrence in 1989 was the presence in the list of semifinalists of four works by women authors: Maria Corti's *Il canto delle sirene*, Paola Capriolo's *Il nocchiero*, Susanna Tamaro's *Una testa fra le nuvole* (A head in the clouds), and Francesca Duranti's *Effetti personali* (Personal effects). In the end, Duranti's novel won the 1989 contest. In 1990, Dacia Maraini's *La lunga vita di Marianna Ucrìa* (The long life of Marianna Ucrìa), and in 1991, Isabella Bossi Fedrigotti's *Di buona famiglia* (Of good family), won the Campiello Prize.

Numerous other prizes—the Rapallo, the Bancarella, the Mondello, the Balzan, the Capri, the Dessí, the Feltrinelli, the Comisso, the Fiuggi, the Pen Club Italiano, etc.—likewise stimulate spectator involvement and encouragement of contestants. The proliferation of literary prizes has not, however, produced a population of voracious readers. A discouraging 1988 statistic reveals that thirty per cent of Italy's inhabitants have never read a book, and in four million Italian homes not a single book may be found.[17]

Chapter Two

Regional Writers and Problems of the South

Caterina Percoto (1812-1887) of Friuli, North Italy, may be considered the forerunner of twentieth-century women writers who reflect the peculiarities of their native regions and concern themselves with the problems of the poor. The story of her life also provides a dramatic example of how the efforts of a gifted woman to assert herself as a writer were mercilessly thwarted by poverty, ill health, and political problems pertinent to the Austrian occupation of northern Italy. Percoto's descriptions of simple farm life in the Friuli-Venezia Giulia region offer a preview of late nineteenth-century *verismo* (see Chapter One, above). Her long and short stories are inspired by the life of the workers and peasants of her region, with whom she felt at one in spirit. Simple feasts, rustic dwellings, muddy fields, primitive plows and smelly chicken coops are described in both Italian and dialect, so realistically that her editors begged her to submit something more imaginative—"more womanly." The wings of Percoto's fancy had, however, early been clipped, and she was too deeply marked by the hardships and misery of her place and time to dissociate herself from the desolate countryside and its broken inhabitants.

Another woman writer of northern Italy whose sorrow and concern for the poor is indelibly impressed in her writings is **Paola Drigo** (1876-1938). Her short veristic novel, *Maria Zef* (1936), describing the brutish life of toilers in the desolate Friuli mountain district, offers a mother-daughter mirror portrait of intense emptiness and despair. A crescendo of pitiful and fearful experiences constitutes the life of the poverty-stricken and now orphaned Mariutine and Rosùte, as of their mother before them. The tragedy of the climax, developing from an interaction of inhuman circumstances and the character of their coal-merchant uncle, Barbe Zef, is further heightened by portraits of father-daughter incest, leading to the closing hatchet-murder scene—all of which combine to make *Maria Zef* a classically constructed and highly moving drama of human disaster.

Painful and distressing existence in Italy's depressed South has not been better described than by two regional women writers, one a Nobel Prize winner, the other a would-be recipient: **Grazia Deledda** (1871-1936) and **Matilde Serao** (1856-1927). The tragic thrust of Deledda's writings and the grim and graphic engravings of Serao's prose in describing the realities of the South and the problems of its people render these two women novelists the most eloquent spokeswomen for the humble folk of the South, who are their closest sisters and brothers. The Swedish Academy, in 1926, was to recognize in Grazia Deledda's work "her power as a writer, sustained by a high ideal, who portrays in plastic forms life as it is on her lonely native island, and who treats problems of general human interest with depth and warmth."[1] Deledda was the second Italian to receive the Nobel distinction after Giosuè Carducci in 1906, and the second woman after Selma Lagerlöf in 1909.

In about fifty stories and novels, Deledda offers readers a richly colored saga of Sardinia, in which characters often reappear (e.g. the servant, Paska; the priest, Elias Portolu; and the author herself as a personage in the narration.)[2] Although thought of today as the playground for the Aga Khan's Emerald Coast jet set, the underpopulated, rugged land, inhabited mainly by austere, primitive shepherds and farmers, is the real Sardinia. If Deledda's forte is the weaving of an exciting story of love, hate, and passion around realistically described characters, it is her even greater contribution to have painted Sardinia's kaleidoscopic nature. Her similes, metaphors, and personifications of lush vegetation and fauna around her native Nuoro, those piercing eyes of her personages, invariably compared to a pair of elements in nature (lizards, stars, etc.), and their keeping of company with the gods that inhabit these natural settings—are as felicitous as they are typically Deleddan.

An unsmiling people of stately bearing, the Sardinians have an innate reservedness and take pride in the antiquity of their race. Despite the widespread banditry that even today mars the island, they are fundamentally shepherds and mountaineers possessed of a keen sense of honor and hospitality. Although Deledda stresses the primitiveness of Sardinian traditions, she always evokes the human aspect of her characters, underlining what is common to all of humankind.

Deledda's early works are concerned mainly with her own interests: family tradition, pride, prejudice, and passion. Against typical settings of wild Sardinian landscapes, her taciturn characters reveal their loneliness and sadness, from which they seek deliverance in an avid search for carnal happiness that is always spoiled by a sense of sin and guilt. The religion of the Sardinians is a fusion of devout Catholicism, atavistic superstitions, witchcraft, pantheism, plus a firm belief in destiny; their dreams are inhabited by ancient mystical events and primitive symbols; and they feel a certain supernatural terror lying somewhere between rigid fatalism and orthodox belief.

On the social level looms the power of the "padrone," met by the sly subservience of servants; women are oppressed and offended; injured families swear vendettas. Further, a perpetual struggle for possession is waged by the islanders—either out of sheer avarice or in an attempt to break the bonds of misery. Passion and psychological conflict, however, in the end exert their supreme influence and account for the behavior of Deledda's literary creatures even more than their economic or social aspirations.

Il vecchio della montagna (The old man of the mountain, 1900), which vividly describes the tragic effects of temptation and the awareness of sin in the conscience of primitive human beings, is the story of a fatal love between an ingenuous youth and a wicked intriguer; *L'edera* (Ivy, 1908) tells of a woman servant who kills in order to save her master from financial ruin but later finds, in marriage with him, nothing but forced expiation for her sin; while *La madre* (*The Mother*, also translated as *The Woman and The Priest*, 1920), is the tragedy of a mother who, with great sacrifice, realizes her dream of her son becoming a priest, only to see him yield to the temptations of the flesh.

Elias Portolu (1903), the drama of a weak man torn between passion and holiness, is considered by many as Deledda's masterpiece and perhaps in no other novel does her mastery of realistic detail and the amazing subtlety and variety of psychological analysis so successfully create the total impression of a life being lived in endless torment. A former convict, the mystically-inclined shepherd Elias, upon returning to his island after having served a prison sentence on the continent, falls in love with his brother's bride. The weak and delicate Elias stands in strong contrast to his robust and manly peasant brother,

Pietro. The former seeks good counsel from a wise old island shepherd, Martinu, who sees in Elias's decision to become a priest a senseless abdication, since the young man's choice of vocation is based not on love for humanity but the simple desire to escape a difficult situation. Elias remains irresolute, fearing to confess his love either to his mother or to his brother. The young bride, Maddelena, unhappy in her relationship with her coarse husband, yields to the temptation of a series of secret rendezvous with her beloved Elias, and ultimately bears his child. The tormented, remorseful Elias now links his love for Maddalena to strong guilt feelings and promptly enters the seminary. His brother, meanwhile, is stricken with a severe kidney infection that causes his death. Maddalena pleas with Elias, who has not yet taken his vows, to become the lawful father of their child, the fruit of their sin. Still lacking the strength to act resolutely, Elias cowers in fear of gossip and negative judgment if he should leave the seminary to marry the woman whom he had nevertheless truly loved. Rejecting Maddalena and entering the priesthood, his next torment is a marriage proposal she has received from one of her wealthy relatives. Maddalena's new husband demonstrates genuine affection for the baby boy, precipitating a crisis of paternal jealousy in Elias, which he is constrained to conceal since the fact that the child is his own is unknown to all except the parents. His affliction, now reduced to silent and desperate love for his son, takes on inordinate proportions of bitterness when the boy dies of intestinal infection. Now, however, a reconciled Elias has won release from vexatious human passions. His soul, prostrate before God, finally gains peace after having tread a long path of sorrow. His lack of resolution had caused a tragic split in his personality. The part given to love and passion is represented in the story by the wise man, Martinu, whose hard life has taught him that one's only salvation is facing situations rather than running from them, that one must place one's own will against destiny, and that one must not fear to follow one's own deep and natural disposition. The part given to insincere or artificial solutions is represented by Prete Porcheddu, the priest who relentlessly goads Elias towards the priesthood, without considering his real inclinations.

  Cenere (*Ashes: A Sardinian Story*, 1904) relates another tormented relationship, this time between a mother and her illegitimate son. The peasant Anania, already married to Tatàna, falls in love with the sixteen-year-old Olì, whom he courts and promises to marry. Olì, turned out of her home by her father because of her pregnancy, bears Anania's child (to whom she gives the name of the father) in the home of a relative, Grathia, where they live in utter misery and solitude, cut off from any contact with Anania. When the child reaches adolescence, however, Olì takes him secretly to Anania's home, where Tatàna lovingly enfolds the unidentified boy, rears him, and provides for his studies. Now a desirable and attractive youth, he is to marry the wealthy young bourgeoise, Margherita, but just before the ceremony, he learns from Grathia that his mother, Olì, who had disappeared after leaving him at his father's home, lives in dire poverty, alone and abandoned. Deciding to sacrifice himself in order to succour his mother, the young man defers the marriage; Olì, thinking to remove the obstacle she is to her son's happiness, commits suicide. The young Anania, opening the amulet that she had hung around his neck in his infancy, finds it contains only ashes. Life indeed now seems to him but ashes for in one fell swoop he has lost his newly found real mother and his would-be bride. Young Anania's unwavering spirit refuses, however, to be crushed. Cherishing hopes that life will again take on substance and solidity, he reaffirms his faith in its gushing force that will carry away the ashes of the dead.

Canne al vento (Reed in the wind, 1913) narrates the decline and fall of an important Sardinian family gnawed by a terrible secret. The life of the servant, Efix, is corroded by an impardonable and deeply painful "sin": he had unintentionally killed his master, the father of a girl he secretly and illicitly loves and whom he had helped escape from her cruel father. To atone in some way for his sin Efix blindly and resignedly works, without pay, for his dead master's daughters, who live in utter solitude and poverty. Efix satisfies his need to expiate his sin by dedicating himself totally to the three sisters, depriving himself of even the basic necessities. Old Efix's pitiful death is the natural conclusion to this tale that so tragically emphasizes the devastating effects of differences in the social scale in Sardinia's primitive society.

This sprinkling of plot summaries should suffice to demonstrate some of the underlying themes in Grazia Deledda's novels, which study so poignantly conflicts between pleasure and duty, will and fatality, crime and punishment. Expiation of sin is an eternal Deleddan theme, and the author seems to be engaged in an unending search for the answer to the tormenting question of whether one must seek the "law" governing one's actions within or outside of one's own person. Humble individuals, through hard sacrifice, attempt to redeem themselves from the scourge of poverty and social unacceptability. How often these attempts are thwarted, however, by temptations, sinful desires, fatal love, diversities of social condition between "padrone" and "servo," intolerance, injustices, humiliations, reciprocal hatreds, sickness and death. Deledda's answer to the evils that beset humankind seems to be contained in a rational "good" that is identified with a moral consciousness guiding human actions. She conceives of life as complex and tormenting, made up of ambiguous and turbid components that fascinate her and at the same time cause her fear. In the end she allows herself to be guided by the modes of her psychological investigation, which she conducts with instinctive simplicity and a tendency to recompose a conditioning moral vision inherited from her own family background. The conservation of an interior and an exterior order, inspired by traditional patterns of Sardinian life, is the prevailing concern of Grazia Deledda, whose renditions of a romantic and idealistic vision captured the attention of the Nobel-Prize jury over half a century ago and continue to intrigue the reader today.

Matilde Serao (1856-1927) is Italy's first woman journalist and one of the most convinced, militant authors in the school of *verismo*. Unofficial candidate for the Nobel Prize in Literature in 1926, she saw her name wiped from the Swedish Academy's slate by the Italian government because of the antimilitarism of her novel, *Mors tua . . .* (1926).

The harsh realities of Italy's depressed South have been discomfortingly described by Serao, who herself knew severe economic restriction during her unhappy childhood. Born in Patras, Greece, to a highly educated Greek mother of noble descent and an Italian father who was an erratically employed journalist in exile, Matilde went to Naples with her parents after the fall of the Bourbon monarchy in 1861. Here she moved in aristocratic circles as well as among the common people of the dark, humid, crumbling buildings in which her literary creatures lived. Serao identified viscerally with the swarming southern city of Naples, which Elsa Morante has described as "the only real Italian metropolis." Serao paints vividly its substandard socio-economic and hygienic conditions, its dark alleyways, its street peddlers, its widespread misery and unemployment. Crime and vice combine in the promiscuity of its overpopulation, and the permanent threat of contagion lurks in this unsanitary inferno where the cholera bacillus nests (and broke out most recently in 1973).

Always personally involved, never ironic or cruel, Serao records graphically her city's misery, melancholy, and manias. Her 1884 publication, entitled *Il ventre di Napoli* (The belly of Naples), comprises nine articles that had appeared in *Capitan Fracassa*, the well-known Roman newspaper whose director had made an exceptional and extraordinary gesture by offering a steady contract to a woman journalist. Through these articles, which contain the seeds of her novels, the reader is made privy to the Naples Serao knew: a city devastated by cholera outbreaks, mass unemployment, and lack of water. Naples lacked a culture worthy of its majestic architecture; its populace senselessly surrendered to the clutches of usurers and the lottery; and the plight of poor, hungry women had reached the lower depths of existence with no ray of sunshine to mitigate their plight. The verbal portrait Serao paints of these lowly women is unforgettable:

> They are thirty but look fifty, they are bent, have lost their hair, their teeth are yellow and black, they walk as though they were lame, they wear a dress for four years and an apron for six months. They don't complain; they don't cry; before they reach the age of forty, they go to die in hospital of malignant fever, pneumonia, or some other horrible disease. And how many of them succomb to cholera! (37).

Bravely, she shouts at government officials, demanding that Naples's greenery be saved, that the city be given more schools, that tourism be increased, that city hall be swept clean of its dishonest politicians, and that crass exploitation of women workers cease. Lovingly, she defends her miserable city—a vital city of intelligent people—which the government of the newly united Italy was relegating to the role of a dead province. The privileges Naples had enjoyed as capital and administrative center of the Kingdom of Two Sicilies were being lost and the area's economy was regressing steadily. Economic interests in north-central Italy were far more protected than those of Italy's impoverished South, from which hundreds of thousands of desperate people emigrated, to the Americas and to France, accepting salaries one-half or one-third less than those paid to workers in northern Italy.

The vociferous journalist does not fear contradicting government officials: " . . . it's not enough to disembowel Naples: practically the whole city needs to be rebuilt" (31). It would be pointless, she argues, to reconstruct three or four of the oldest, most fetid parts of the city. A total remaking of the city was needed, with appropriate social and economic reforms. Time has proven Serao to be right. A partially disemboweled Naples still sees its problems of unemployment, housing, and civic and social reforms unsolved even today. Motorbikes and cars crowd the narrow streets, along which sad-eyed old women sell bootleg cigarettes; girls huddle around a worktable in a dark basement, assembling cheap gold jewelry for one of hundreds of small subcontractors that make up Naples's business fabric. Still today, Neapolitans say, Naples has three times as many garbage collectors as Paris and three times as much uncollected garbage on the streets.[3] Serao's works denouncing injustices done to the city of Naples still have contemporary force. Her concerns of nearly a century ago remain unanswered. The buildings constructed in place of those demolished are inevitably occupied by offices or apartments for the lower-middle or middle classes, while the poor go to resettle in the city's old quarters, aggravating the problems already existing there. The composite emblem on the cover of a relatively recent edition of *Il ventre di Napoli* is a cluster of rats, setting the tone for the content of the book. Nor has Naples yet found a viable solution to its rat proliferation problem, as borne out by the multiple official extermination notices posted in the city's various zones, including, ironically, in the very square that bears the name of Matilde Serao.[4]

Vita e avventure di Riccardo Joanna (Life and adventures of Riccardo Joanna, 1887) and *Il paese di cuccagna* (Land of plenty, 1891), are two of Serao's veristic novels that focus on the misery of Neapolitan life, observed firsthand and imprinted indelibly on the reader's mind: intolerable living conditions of qualified workers and artisans; incredibly low salaries of newspaper typographers; pressing needs for more decent surroundings, adequate sleeping arrangements, better food and clothing, and thirst for human affection.

The first part of *Vita e avventure di Riccardo Joanna* relates the tribulations of the widower, Paolo, a journalist struggling in Naples to make ends meet for himself, his child, Riccardo, and his simpleminded housekeeper from the Campania province. Paolo grubs incessantly in order to pay the rent for the room in which all three live. His face, with its monotonous, almost hebetudinous expression of fatigue, is hauntingly described by Serao, as are the figures of the wretched, underpaid employees of the newspaper office and printshop, who carry on their work despite constant deafening noise around them. The stultifying work of the newspaper employees, which reduces them to silent, arid individuals, is compared by Serao to that of peasants who, after hours of hoeing the ground under a scorching sun or a driving rain, are reduced, at the end of the day, to an almost animal desire for food—food that consists of nothing more than a bowl of potato-and-beetroot soup. Vividly described also are the malnourished street urchins who gather each day to receive the newspapers they will peddle through the streets of Naples: first, however, they must learn from the distributor, through rote repetition, what headline to shout, since they themselves cannot read.

Paolo struggles, anxiously and impatiently, to meet deadlines, undergoing long hours of mental concentration and daily sacrifice, which produce at the end of each day an undermining low grade fever. Neglect and malnourishment have as their consequence Paolo's contraction first of bronchitis, then of pneumonia, which results in his early death—a serene and august death, however, for despite his physical weakness, he has worked up to the last days of his life. His colleagues and the newspaper director contribute alms for the funeral expenses, and the latter obtains a clerical job for Paolo's penniless young son, Riccardo, at a government ministry in Rome, where poverty nonetheless continues to stalk him. Balking at the routine clerical work and the horribly bad food which are his fare, Riccardo, "in whose veins flows printer's ink," gives up his job in order to face the challenges of the newspaper world, despite the vow he had made to the dying Paolo not to follow his father's métier. Riccardo each day faces new problems of survival. In the end, he is unable to escape the misery and oppression that fatally plague him and the people of Naples.

The ironic title of what is considered Matilde Serao's masterpiece, *Il paese di cuccagna*, focuses on another Neapolitan scourge: that sickness, that passion, that vice that is the lottery, which takes possession of all, from the humblest miscreant to the highest magistrate. The game, it is thought, offers a unique opportunity to right the wrongs of birth, poverty, and status through some magnificent stroke of luck, through a challenge to fate. With considerable wry humor, Serao describes how, in a land of misery, the debased populace, aspiring to "meat and macaroni," deprives itself of its daily crust of bread in order to save enough to purchase a lottery ticket for each Saturday's drawing of the winning numbers. Given the impossibility of finding steady, remuneratory work, the Neapolitans perform a multitude of odd and underpaid jobs, from which they set aside their weekly gambling costs. An unhappy people, without homes, without refuge, and plagued by hunger, they nevertheless always manage to put together a few coins to gamble. Those who do have jobs, the women employed in a nauseating tobacco factory, for example, work seven days a week, but cannot afford to eat or dress decently since they must provide for the unemployed members of their families, and the few lire remaining in their pockets must inexorably be spent on gambling.

Intensifying the chronic inanition of Naples's miserable population, Serao provides a full-page description (39) of a tray of multicolored pastries and sherbets being served at a christening party in the home of a wealthy family. This mouth-watering reading experience goes far in sharpening the reader's vicarious experience of Neapolitan yearning and gives full flavor to the savory "land of plenty" over the rainbow—the goal of all of Naples's gamblers. Usury, pawnbroking, sorcery, wizardry, and witchcraft flourish in the bowels of Naples, where the lottery fever spreads relentlessly among both the poor and the decadent nobility.

Il paese di cuccagna pivots, in fact, on the tragic household of the Marquis Cavalcanti, descendant of the great thirteenth-century Florentine poet and friend of Dante Alighieri, Guido Cavalcanti. This illustrious household is falling into ruin, dishonor, and death (first his wife's, then his daughter's) because of the Marquis's lottery craze. Serao's descriptions of the demented nobleman's fixation is worthy of the pen of Molière: he aspires to a great fortune and, to achieve his goal, he spurs his hypersensitive daughter into ritualistic trances that will supply him the necessary "revelations" for choosing the winning lottery numbers. Hanging on to her every word spoken in trance, he uses her unrelentlessly as each lottery drawing day approaches. The meek, submissive Bianca Maria, overexcited by her father's goadings, becomes more and more subject to fever, delirium, hallucinations, and convulsions, as her father mercilessly forces her to communicate with the "spirit"—the spirit that denotes, for him, revelation, but in reality signifies the spirit of death. Whenever he holds his cabbalistic meetings with friends in the living room of the bare Cavalcanti mansion (whose furnishings have been sold to pay for losing lottery tickets), Bianca Maria huddles in prayer, with their unpaid servant, in her cold bedroom, reciting the rosary tremulously. No longer the Marquis's flesh and blood daughter, Bianca Maria has become a mere intermediary between her father and elusive fortune.

General delirium takes hold of the city's population each Saturday, as each gambler "spera nella vincita e dispera della vincita" (hopes to win and despairs of ever winning; the play on the words *sperare* and *disperare* is lost in English translation but is analogous to "Man never is, but always to be, blest," the rhyming verset of Alexander Pope's well-known line: "Hope springs eternal in the human breast"). Serao describes the Neapolitan gambler's contradictory emotions with dosed persiflage: willful determination never to gamble again is mixed in equal proportion with fanciful imaginings of having won that day's lottery game.

Cavalcanti's continual proddings ultimately lead to the wasted Bianca Maria's demise. Repentant father, the Marquis kneels at her deathbed, stretching out his arms to ask pardon. (Serao likens him to an old King Lear seeking forgiveness from sweet Cordelia.) The city of Naples continues, however, to plunge ever more deeply into despair, and its misery assumes ever more tragic overtones as extreme degradation perverts even the most aristocratic of families. Mortals who dream of winning the lottery fall into lethargy and idleness. Like all visions, glittering winnings are propped on deceptions and lies. Like all hallucinations, the hope of winning leads to cruelty and ferocity. Like all false remedies that arise from poverty, the lottery produces only more poverty, degradation, and crime. "The Neapolitans," writes Serao, "a sober people, are not addicted to alcohol, nor do they die from *delirium tremens*; they become addicted and die from the lottery. The lottery is Naples's alcohol" (*Il ventre di Napoli*, 61).

Naples is likewise the setting for Viareggio-Prize-winning *Il mare non bagna Napoli* (*The Bay Is Not Naples*, 1953), by **Anna Maria Ortese** (1915-   ), one of Italy's best representatives of neorealism.[5] Together with a group of post-World War II Neapolitan writers, Ortese did much to replace bourgeois literature with the literature of the people, focusing national and international attention on problems of the South, with which, however, her relationship (unlike Serao's) is strictly literary. Ortese's interest is in the striking contrast between the bright turquoise of the Mediterranean and the deep sadness of its people. If she and her group describe with neorealistic blackness the despair of Neapolitans, they concomitantly make a parallel profession of cultural and literary faith. In the name of reason and citizenship, they are determined, as Neapolitan writers, to upset and destroy false myths about their city and give poetic expression to a truer social and moral portrait of a people and a district.

Ortese smashes clichés of the picturesque city on the bay crowned by a smoldering Mount Vesuvius, and causes flickers of legendary ebullience and *joie de vivre* fitfully to burn out. Like Serao, she attempts to discredit and overturn commonplace images of conventional society and move her readers away from folkloristic unrealities. She would like to restore to Naples its real face, different from the one presented by the ancient and modern classics.[6] The passivity, patience, and sentimentalism of Neapolitans thus lose their charm and become, under Ortese's pen, negative traits that cause them and their city to fall into stagnation. The true visage of the Neapolitan is not the singing, smiling, enchanting mask making merry in street processions, but rather an unhappy, sick, coarse figure deprived of his "meat and macaroni."

The Bay Is Not Naples, a realistic and autobiographical chronicle of Ortese's experiences, made its midcentury readers uncomfortable. Her drastic message disturbed Italian complacency, for it reads like an accusation leveled against an entire social system that had permitted the total degradation of an unfortunate, pockmarked sector of its population. In the crudest of terms, Ortese plots the trajectory of Naples's absurd and headlong fall, while the rest of Italian hypocritical society looks on indifferently. Her descriptions of the devastated city, steeped in squalor and age-old ills, demonstrated that the general socioeconomic progress made during the 1950s had never reached the South. Ortese's chronicle, although it exudes pity, ire, and scorn, at the same time recognizes that exaggerated family affection, sentimentalism, and instincts have obfuscated the Neapolitans' rationality and awareness, thereby permitting poverty and misery to ascend and triumph. Torn and lacerated figures, they are evocative of certain eternal masks of the *commedia dell'arte*: unruly, disorderly, and disheveled, yet at the same time inspiring in the spectator a feeling for their underlying dignity and resiliency.

Ortese's Naples is a city populated by a sub-proletariat stricken with a high rate of syphilis and a tuberculosis rate of ninety per cent affected or susceptible to infection. Neapolitan children, many of whom suffer rickets, witness their parents' copulation in their overcrowded hovels, and repeat the gestures as a game, for lack of any other distraction. The author's creatively imaginative description of the city's horrendous "granili," where homeless human beings live like a colony of insects in a Kafkaesque setting, succeeds in piercing the hardest of hearts. Hallucinating and surrealistic, the "granili" are a "demonstration, in clinical and juridical terms, of the decline of a species," writes Ortese. These citizens "are no longer Neapolitans, nor anything else" (63, 68).

The first episode in *The Bay Is Not Naples* is symbolic of the cruelty in Neapolitan life: an almost blind child places all her hopes for change, happiness and a better life, on a pair of eyeglasses that cost the exorbitant price, for her poverty-stricken family, of "eight thousand lire"—the leitmotiv of the chapter. Once the glasses are on her nose, however, suddenly her ragged, deformed and pockmarked neighbors seem to lunge at her out of the dim shadows in which she had been accustomed to seeing them. What her corrected vision shows her is a hitherto unknown surrealistic world that causes the girl to be overcome by nausea and vomiting and to fling the eyeglasses away in rejection. Gone are her illusions, as well as the eight thousand lire. Having opened her eyes to a frightening world of horrors, different from the comfortable haziness she knew, the poor myopic child has symbolically experienced existential nausea.

Suffering and squalor are unremittingly presented by Ortese with bitter realism, neorealism, and even grotesque surrealism. To these, however, she lends a humanistic balance, aimed at creating a new, authentic vision of life in which humankind's dormant sensibilities may be released. Faithful narrations of the crudest facts of life and sensitivity to the harsh dramatic realities of socio-civic problems are offset by fantasy, imagination and an ability to transform reality into dream or hallucination, in a magic-fantastical style that furnishes the key for entering the domain of *L'iguana* (*The Iguana*, 1965), Ortese's most important novel.

A "theological" fable, *The Iguana* is filled with pages of surprises unfolding in gentle settings, spiked by picaresque adventures without any narrative logic. Perhaps this horn-shaped island of Ocaña where the humanized iguana lives is Ortese's escape from the horrors of Neapolitan reality. She takes the reader back to times remote, to archaic, idyllic, peaceful landscapes that are perhaps a transposition of the *locus amoenus* that Naples was in a distant past. Perhaps some of the ugly, inhuman-looking cast of characters in the city's slums, with their absent glances and their myopic expression, but who never-

theless have souls in their grotesque bodies, are the embryo of
the Ocaña residents. Certainly, the seven-year-old girl in *The
Bay Is Not Naples*, who looks, dresses and acts like a lady but like
an animal too, who curtsies and then spits (119-120), is the proto-
type of the enigmatic human iguana, with her inherent features
of both queen and serf.

The Iguana is an illustration of Ortese's definition of man
as "someone who lives in a place that is not his." The universe,
for her, seems to be the real Unreal, or the unreal Real, the un-
thinkable and unthought of place where nature takes on human
attributes. The island of Ocaña is where the human being, toler-
ated by an invasive nature, can recognize itself as part of nature
and as part of the island. In this way, Ortese permits the
Neapolitan to find and reassert his identity, and thereby regain
his/her charm and capacity to move, for "like all monstrosities,
Naples made no impression on scarcely human persons, and its
immeasurable charms could leave no trace on a cold heart" (*The
Bay Is Not Naples*, 158).

The iguana is humankind without the defense of rational
intelligence, without concepts of time—humankind that
dreams. It is bizarre youth that sees itself as beautiful, healthy,
happy, and is full of optimism and joy, even though aware that
the future is far off and perhaps not even its own. Ortese's fable,
akin to García Marquez's magic realism in which fantasy, myth,
and literary illusions alternate with naturalism, gives impetus to
the dramatic aspects of the questions raised by the ambiguities of
contemporary society. Thus, the novel deserves to be read and
interpreted by all, each in his or her own way.

If Ortese's iguana is an illumination in nature, and if the
island of Ocaña is where humankind can recognize itself as part
of nature, then little Arturo, and the island of Procida[7] in the Bay
of Naples are, similarly, their mythical counterparts as conceived
by **Elsa Morante** (1912-1985), the adolescent Arturo representing
destiny and his island absolute time and space. Having once
established that Procida is situated off the coast of the South's
largest city, the reader may now be assured that Morante's magical realism precludes identification of Arturo's island with any
specific geographical location. Rather, it is the golden, sonorous
place where Arturo's parents lived, where he spent his childhood and experienced his first life sensations, made his first discoveries, knew happiness and then lost it. *L'isola di Arturo*
(*Arturo's Island*, 1957, Strega Prize 1966), Morante's most accessi-
ble and obvious novel, must find its definition somewhere be-

tween symbolism and neorealism, halfway between mythical fable and Neapolitan dialectical regionalism. The story of Arturo—like that of the iguana—unfolds in a sure movement between reality and fantasy, between myth and chronicle, and the sixteen years of the protagonist's life on Procida are like sixteen years of sleep, far removed from the events in the world.

Although the universality of Elsa Morante's writings preclude a classification of the author as a "regional writer," still all of her novels are either set in the South or have a southern starting point or destination: *Arturo's Island* in Procida (Naples); *House of Liars* (see Chapter Four, below) in a dusty town of both legendary and modern Sicily, where the meridional setting is used by the author to denounce certain situations inherent in the Sicilian life style; *La Storia* (*History: A Novel*), the tragic story of a Calabrian woman in Rome during World War II (see Chapter Three, below); and *Aracoeli*, which takes the reader to a dusty village in southern Spain (see Chapter Four, below). Although the scope of *Arturo's Island* goes well beyond regionalism and neorealism, and its theme revolves around the initiation rites of a boy up the moment of his shedding of childish myths to pass into the disenchanting realities of the adult world, the novel will be treated here for its southern local color.

Born into poverty in Rome, of a Sicilian father who was an instructor in a reform school for minors, and a northern Italian mother, a schoolteacher, Elsa Morante spent her childhood in the noisy, picturesque section of Rome known as Testaccio, without attending grammar school and living most of her day in happy, quarrelsome contact with the street urchins of the neighborhood. Anarchical and anticonformist, she remained essentially an autodidact, a rebel, and an affectionate accomplice of that strata of society she knew too well: abandoned children, the downtrodden and oppressed—all the disinherited of the earth. Later, leaving her parents' home, she went to live in the villa of a wealthy godmother. Obviously the life style in that villa aroused Elsa's equivocal scorn and attraction to luxury and opulence, which remained with her for the rest of her life. Returning to her parents' home in order to finish her studies at the *liceo*, Morante subsequently took up residence alone, short of money, and failing to assert herself as a writer. In one of the two most significant dreams recorded in her *Diary 1938*, Elsa, searching for a "room of her own" and finding a bed for rent in the humble kitchen of an old woman who spends most of her time cooking, reluctantly rejects the not unpleasant "bed for let" as scarcely the suitable place for creative writing. Her marriage to Alberto Moravia in 1941 alleviated her difficulties and opened to her wider horizons and new opportunities. Her active participation in a lively literary circle, supplemented by inexhaustible curiosity for contemporary Italian authors as well as for Cervantes, Stendhal, and the metaphysical painters (especially Giorgio de Chirico and his brother, Albert Savinio), were important influences in her work, but Morante always skillfully skirted the circle of her cultural counterparts. Her natural inclination was to combine a taste for fairy tales, magic, and the baroque with a personal language inspired by metaphysical values.

Morante's long sojourn (1941-43) in Anacapri atop the island of Capri brought her into contact with many of the legends, myths, and poetic evocations that were to find expression in her magic realism. Subsequently, she was compelled to leave Rome, in 1943, during German occupation of the capital, taking precarious refuge in the countryside near Cassino (south central Italy), the city that was completely destroyed during World War II and remembered today for the American bombing of its historical Benedictine monastery. Her exile here, in an eternal search for food, allowed her to make further discoveries about the world of the South and aroused in her affectionate admiration for its people, whose linguistic and dialectical peculiarities fascinated her. (Some of them are reproduced in *Arturo's Island.*)

A wild, only child, weaned on goat's milk and raised in absolute freedom on the relatively untouched island of Procida, Arturo relates, in the first person, his childhood and his memories. His mother had died in childbirth at the hands of a midwife—a common occurrence in this milieu—but her soul remains personified as Arturo's "queen" *in absentia*. The wonder of his growth into manhood is purposely set by the author in a turquoise sea, from which all life on this planet originally emerged, and the earthly paradise of Procida serves as the backdrop for the living out of a simple life. Arturo, like most Neapolitans and other southerners, enjoys sitting outside his home at night, contemplating the firmament that assumes the proportions of a vast body of water, and listening to the sounds of the sea, his play companion that would, like him, grow up and carry him off to the great ocean, to exotic lands, and to all other adventures. Procida's inspiring landscape is marred only by an imposing building set high on a cliff dominating the island: the penitentiary, a symbol of the shutting off from life and love of those criminals who, for Morante, are nothing but the outgrowth and the victims of poverty and social imbalances.

The descriptions of the island are realistic and detailed, yet mythical, metaphorical, and magical. Around the port area, narrow streets never see the sun; crudely built, crumbling, rustic buildings huddle together, and though painted in soft pastel colors, they are sad and severe. Their windows are like narrow loopholes, whose sills support carnations planted in old tin cans, or tiny cages big enough for crickets perhaps but crushing for the captive turtledoves they contain. The shops in these buildings are deep and dark, like the dens of thieves; the taciturn islanders are closed in silent diffidence and ill temper, even though the island is so luminous, so Mediterranean, so Homeric. Women live cloistered, like nuns; it is considered sinful for them to seabathe or even look at others bathing; at dusk, Procida's women observe the tacit curfew and retire to their homes closing themselves up physically and mentally behind their shutters. Morante stresses the darkness in which these southern women live, and their exclusion from any meaningful social life, through her description of the palatial residence of Romeo l'Amalfitano—an eerie mansion which had originally been a monastery, then a military barracks, and finally an exclusive domain from which women had systematically been excluded.

Arturo's home—gray and vile as opposed to the glitter of the sunny sea and the twinkling of the starry firmament— conveys an oppressive and decaying atmosphere: it is dirty, filled with rubble, and its closets that smell of "defunct Bourbon bourgeoisie" serve only to receive the worthless junk that gives the bedrooms their characteristic odor of boats and grottoes. Since neither Arturo nor his knight-errant father spend very much time in the house, spiders, lizards, birds, bats, and all the island's nonhuman creatures, considering it uninhabited, visit frequently and freely, in lieu of human callers. Even though Arturo's home is in the thickly inhabited part of the island, around it "solitude traces an enormous space, evil and marvelous, like a golden cobweb" (15).

The human characters in the novel are even more poignantly delineated. Arturo and his vagrant father, Wilhelm Gerace, illegitimate son of an islander and a German woman, dress in the same clothing all year round, with neither the bother nor the benefit of any form of underwear. Each possesses two sweaters, worn one over the other in winter time for warmth. Despite these apparent privations, Arturo's childhood unfolds like a happy landscape, in which he is king of Procida, his father—incarnation of human greatness—reigns supreme as his god, and a simple black sea urchin constitutes the most splendid of nature's gifts. The first sense of revolt against life's order is felt by Arturo only when, turning fourteen, he learns from his father that he is about to acquire a "new mother." For Arturo, whose only mother can be his oriental "queen," his "siren of the sea" whose golden canary voice guides him back whenever he swims too far out from shore, the news is both shocking and abhorrent. His repugnance is reinforced by the sight of his Neapolitan stepmother disembarking in the port of Procida: awkward, ugly, exuberant, and grotesque in her high heels, the bewildered Nunziata conveys the impression that "she had reached Baghdad or Istanbul" (76).

One out of ten children, Nunziata, Wilhelm Gerace's newly chosen wife, poverty-stricken herself and full of pity for the downtrodden, is minutely and pathetically described by Morante. By accepting marriage to Gerace, she has gained release from a sordid existence in the slums of Naples, where her entire family lived, slept, and cooked in one room, in which strands of homemade pasta could be hung over the bedsprings to dry, and in which a cooking hotplate, set on the doorstep in summer, served as portable kitchen the year round. Devout to the point of superstition, Nunziata has brought to the island, in her half-empty suitcase, several images of the various Madonnas in which she firmly believes, together with her few faded, dirty items of apparel. She tightly clutches a purse containing her wealth: trinkets and trifles that Wilhelm will subsequently, spitefully and brutally, strew on the ground, in the first of many illustrations of Nunziata's silent and pious subjection to her husband's moods and violence.

Two weeks after bringing his bride to Procida, Wilhelm, whose precious presence has been enjoyed by both Arturo and Nunziata, once again announces his imminent departure from the island. Arturo is convinced that the knight-errant is off to adventurous, noble and heroic actions, but Nunziata, who knows the terrible truth of Wilhelm's sordid homosexual involvements, tries to detain him. Returning in less than a week, Wilhelm brings to Nunziata two cheap gifts, and offers nothing to Arturo except a fifty-lire piece. Realizing his father has returned to the island not for his son, but for Nunziata, Arturo's sublimations of his father and interest in his peregrinations quickly wane. He begins to feel the uselessness of his own presence in the household. Overcome by a sense of emptiness and desperation, he is inevitably attracted towards the ebullient Nunziata.

The entire part of the book devoted to the genesis of Arturo's sexual desires is an exquisitely wrought description of an incestuous yet innocent attachment, in which Arturo wakens to love through natural instincts, and spontaneously shares his joy with nature. "The difficult subjects of homosexuality and incest are treated naturally," writes one critic, "with delicacy and realism, permitting Arturo's drama to remain the drama of a young boy."[8]

Thus, in *Arturo's Island*, Elsa Morante demonstrates her infinite capacity to dispose of and manipulate to perfection all the new values of Italy's neorealistic literary language and narrative structures. If her inner world was inhabited by the joyous images of Arturo's island, she also was sensitive to the demented psychological atmosphere that pervaded the island of Sicily with its characteristic hostile prejudices, rivalries, and vendettas (cf. *House of Liars*, Chapter Four, below). Certainly it was not Naples and its surroundings but more likely her Sicilian heritage that caused her to see the outside world as blinded by hatred rather than by love. From that world, she sought escape through what she had facetiously called her "autoeuthanasia." Little did she realize that her suicide attempt and later death served only to impoverish even further her beloved South, and all of Italy too, for the magic wand that was her pen is irreplaceable and Italian literature is immeasurably poorer for the loss of Elsa Morante from the ranks of its "scrittori."

* * *

[Don Lucio's] clothing had been brushed and folded . . . and his highly polished shoes had been placed on the stool so that he would not have to bend to get them. . . . Nicolina waited humbly until he finished washing [his face after shaving] in order to hand him the towel . . . then she brought him his toothbrush [and] . . . combed his hair. . . . She buttered the white bread (. . . for him alone) and poured the milk, not too hot and not too cold. As he ate . . . she continued serving him. . . . From the moment she got up in the morning—and she rose when it was still dark—up to late at night, she did not allow herself a moment's rest. She was the one who . . . ironed, cooked . . . remained standing during meals, even though her legs trembled from fatigue, ready to

> change his plate . . . pour his wine, peel his fruit . . . fill
> his pipe . . . prepare his warm lemon-drink . . . Nicolina
> [was] attached to the house like thick lichen attaches
> itself to reef. . . .[9]

Thus does **Maria Messina** (1887-1944) describe the consideration accorded to the patriarchal figure of Don Lucio in her Sicilian novel *La casa nel vicolo* (The house in the narrow street, 1921). Called "the Sicilian Katherine Mansfield" by Italy's well-known author, the late Leonardo Sciascia, Messina delineates realistically, in her tales and novels, the position of women in Sicilian society up to the years of World War II. She describes their oppression and suffering as they live out their existence in appalling southern domestic settings, where women themselves hope their babies will be born boys, because "women are born to serve and to suffer. For nothing else" (65). Messina's secluded women characters are imprisoned or cloistered in a monotonous family existence, their thoughts and feelings reduced to silence. In their large homes with little light, they seem relieved and breathe more freely when the patriarchs are absent, yet they fear to confess their alleviation openly. The hours pass slowly—"always the same, always heavy" on the hands and heart.

Like her devoted correspondent, Giovanni Verga, Messina sees Sicilian life in its crudest nakedness, in its misery and poverty, and in its obstinate melancholy without any streaks of lush landscape nor dramatic bloodshed such as one finds in Grazia Deledda's works. Her scenes of Sicilian life are all in a minor key. The honest but miserable people she describes enter and exit from life unobtrusively, and have enough decorum to hush their cries of anguish. But their repressed and tenacious sorrow manifests itself in a way more awful than a deep tragedy or a disastrous downfall. In Sicily, Messina informs her readers, thousands of honest, petty landowners and small professionals languish and lose their vigor in the face of unending financial preoccupations. Their penury suffocates every sentiment except that of resigned sacrifice and fear of God. Young girls brought up to believe that they must marry a prince charming in their teens because later they are no longer desirable, may be found pining in their dimly lit chambers as they ply their sewing needles in tempo with a monotonous existence of hoping and waiting. Sicily's unlimited patriarchy, in which a father is dispensed from any accounting of his actions or absences and is permitted to inflict corporal punishment on his children and demand subservience form his wife, combine to produce a semilethargic life style unduplicated anywhere else in Italy (except, perhaps, in Calabria). The ravaging effects and the moral devastation brought about by Sicily's traditions and conventions are effectively described by Maria Messina, who herself knew the sunless life of the petty bourgeoisie who live out a senseless existence behind tightly closed windows and shutters that will not fail to remind the reader of García Lorca's house of Bernarda Alba.

Don Lucio, the patriarch in *La casa nel vicolo*, is complacent and self-righteous. A scrupulous administrator, he is at the same time a ruthless moneylender, who justifies his usury as a means to enrich his daughters and render them marriageable. Don Lucio lords it over two sisters: his wife, the spineless Antonietta, who obeys his every whim, and her sister, Nicolina, who is essentially a servant in their household, and with whom Lucio takes his pleasure from time to time, when his wife is indisposed, despite Nicolina's trembling protests. As for his three children, Lucio's little whip tucked into the back of his chair is sufficient threat to keep them physically silent and mentally obedient. Since Lucio must work with his head, his sleep cannot be sacrificed as can that of insignificant women. Antonietta and Nicolina, therefore, continually move about the house awkwardly and automatistically, victims of the mysterious inviolability of Don Lucio's sleep.

Rarely if ever do the women go out into the streets of their town, which is considered a frivolous demonstration of oneself; moreover, cloistering reduces expenses of dresses and shoes. After the death of their father, in fact, the two sisters have closed themselves hermetically inside the house in the narrow street, and their "mourning that continues for years and years is a good way [for Don Lucio] to save money" (40).

When their young son, Alessio, falls victim to typhoid fever, only *in extremis* does Don Lucio allow a physician to enter his house: "The sole thought that a strange man should enter his home . . . made him extremely uncomfortable" (41). Once the diagnosis is pronounced by the medical doctor, Lucio, fearful of contagion, leaves his wife and sick child in the master bedroom and moves into the living room to sleep and eat alone for the duration of Alessio's illness. The boy's recovery leaves the father totally apathetic. When the lad damages a rented bicycle and Don Lucio is asked by his wife to pay for the repair, he refuses, referring to Alessio as "your son" who gives his father nothing but bitter bread to bite. Lucio's indifference, harshness, and cruelty, together with Alessio's discovery that he is a usurer, lead to the young boy's suicide, precipitating his mother's insanity—like that of so many mothers in novels dealing with the South.[10] Antonietta, communicating with holy images and the souls of the departed, begins having hallucinations of her dead son and in the darkness of her room, "among the soft folds of her black shawl, her face seemed to appear, bodiless, like the apparition of a ghost" (134).

Don Lucio, instead, seizes every opportunity to inculcate additional fears into his daughters who are now pale, thin, and clothed in long black dresses that contrast cruelly with the bright Sicilian sunshine they are forced to flee. He goes so far as to withdraw them from school, for "he wanted to keep them in his custody. He wanted to educate them himself, in his own way, to be docile, simple, ignorant, without desires, as befits women" (137). Messina's indignation is strong but scarcely expressed. Her attempts to explain Don Lucio's immorality and cruelty of character are halfhearted. It is true that his childhood had been poor, lonely, hard, and bitter; that he had been the victim of beatings from a grandfather who had first raised him and then turned him out of the house; that his present heart condition gives him grave concern. These explanations are watered down and unconvincing, however, for Maria Messina honestly cannot muster sympathy nor find sufficient justification for the personage of the Sicilian patriarch.

After the tragedy of Alessio's suicide, life resumes its usual course in the dark house in the narrow street, whose image, throughout the novel, is opposed to the serenity and openness of the distant sea and skies and the stars in their infinity. Old habits are again taken up, carried out mechanically, and each person continues living out the deep solitude within his or her soul. The dark house in the narrow street is a metaphor for the entire island of Sicily. It is nothing but an old ship, quickly swallowed by the darkness of the night, rotting in a port delineated by the Straits of Messina and the Gulf of Tunis, and whose passengers have never seen the horizon because they spend their heavy, silent hours locked inside their cabins.

Sicily is once again the real protagonist in the more modern novels, *L'inferriata* (The iron grating, 1976), by **Laura Di Falco** (1910-   ), a Sicilian-born journalist, novelist, and painter; *Volevo i pantaloni* (I wanted pants, 1989) by **Lara Cardella** (see Chapter Seven, below); **Luisa Adorno**'s *Arco di luminara* (Illuminated arch), 1990); and **Dacia Maraini**'s *La lunga vita di Marianna Ucrìa* (The long life of Marianna Ucrìa, 1990).

The young heroine of *L'inferriata*, the novel that finished in third place for the Strega Prize in 1976, is only a symbol of the town of Ortigia, where human desires, emotions, and aspirations are all sacrificed to the fear of scandal. Choked by the hypocrisy of the petty bourgeois in her pitiless society, Diletta must fend off cries of scandal and surrender to her town's moral code of compromise. Having been taken by surprise by the police during a clandestine rendezvous in an automobile with a boyfriend, Mario, Diletta is forced to submit to a hastily arranged reparatory engagement, Mario having accepted to play the game of conventions and prejudices of the inhabitants of Ortigia. At the end of the novel, an explosion of inflammable liquid stored in a tanker docked in one of the many industrial plants that have invaded and degraded the Sicilian coastline, provides the precipitating element for Diletta's crucial decision: whether to flee Ortigia forever to seek a less hostile mode of living, or to stay on, continue to compromise, and face courageously the problems of *her* South.

Adorno's autobiographical *Arco di luminara*, which won the Viareggio Prize in 1990, tells of the hustle and bustle of four generations in her husband's Sicilian home. She, a Pisan, lives out suppressed anger at the condition of women in this "*ultima provincia*" (last province), the title of her 1962 autobiographical novel. Adorno is cruel to herself as she describes her sprawling in a grotesque fall, or her submissive acceptance in sewing a button when she is really too sleepy. Taken advantage of by both her husband and their maid, the chagrined heroine recognizes that she lives her life "without dignity."

Dacia Maraini's *La lunga vita di Marianna Ucrìa*, winner of the 1990 Campiello Prize, is set in eighteenth-century aristocratic Palermo. Because the heroine is a deaf-mute, and a burden to her noble family, she is married off to an old, irascible, and egotistic uncle, forced to bear him five children, but never receives a word of love, tenderness, or understanding. It is only through her own intelligence, sensitivity, and astuteness that Marianna succeeds in transforming the silent void in which she lives into a meaningful world of her own.

Livia De Stefani (1913-   ) is the Sicilian author who gained notoriety for her 1953 novel, *La vigna delle uve nere* (The black-grape vineyard), deprecated by some as outlandish and scabrous, and praised by others for its moving quality and its basic lyricism. Considered a "classic" in Italy, the novel is the recital of a tragic, incestuous love in the heart of Sicily—a region, like Sardinia, known for the primitive passions and dark dramas of its inhabitants. Coldly received in Sicily, *La vigna delle uve nere* was acclaimed on the continent and abroad—especially in the Nordic countries, where it was widely translated. By way of explanation of the novel's success outside of Sicily, De Stefani referred to her native island as "a well full of miracles, from which all the stories drawn diffuse a mythological scent that captivates readers of the most disparate latitudes and origins."[11]

The myth contained in *La vigna delle uve nere* is closely related to the divine presuppositions of Greek tragedy, which had strongly marked the island of Sicily in ancient times, and in which guilt/chastisement, or crime/punishment, or more broadly, life/death play reciprocal and almost inseparable roles.[12] A dour peasant family is dominated by the coarse and massive presence of the father, Casimiro Badalamenti, whose vulgar and insensitive companion, Concetta, will become his wife only late in life and solely for opportunistic reasons of power and convenience in his old age. Their two children, Nicola and Rosaria, are poetic, sensitive, fable-like beings, who had lived their childhood away from home, entrusted to the care of a money-thirsty couple, since the conditioned Casimiro's sense of honor forbade him from recognizing his illegitimate offspring. After the late marriage of Concetta and Casimiro, Nicola and Rosaria are brought into the Badalamenti household, where lack of any tender attachment on the part of the parents (who had refused earlier to bring them into public view) now presses the siblings together, as they clutch for some form of surrogate affection. Their loneliness and sense of abandonment draw them spiritually and physically closer; their father's punishment of Nicola (casting him into chains) is met by Rosaria's running with the "rustle of doves' wings" to comfort her brother each night, unmindful of the danger and the sin involved. The sexual act these primordial creatures perform is the celebration of a ritual that takes on tones of innocence and sublimity, but the fatal consequence will be the murder of the two "sinners" by their father. The horrendous relationship and the impious act must be expiated. They docilely accept the death decree uttered with the voice of divine authority by the priest-executioner who is arbiter of life and death.[13] Casimiro's original rejection and later malediction of his children are destined to be played out in an expiation rite of idyllic love and tragic death, in which incest is both punishment and redemption.

* * *

Although almost all of the novels that have been considered in the foregoing pages date back several decades, the life
of many Italian women of the South still remains strongly
anchored in archaic structures. A preponderant number of
southern women continue to play traditional roles, and their
condition is still backward in a society where stagnant under-
development prevails. Ignorant and often illiterate, they do
obscure work and have unwanted children. In the South, the
employment rate of women is only 25 per cent as compared to
33.6 per cent in the North (1989 statistics), and work, often
perceived as a perpetuation of Biblical malediction, rarely helps
to improve the social awareness and status of southern women.
Essentially, they remain socially rather than biologically
discriminated against, and have yet to find fertile soil on the
sunny islands of Sicily and Sardinia in which to plant seeds for
their self-realization and fulfillment of their aspirations.

Chapter Three

The Historical Novel

Roman and Italian history, in which the role of feminine forces is relatively limited, has nevertheless exerted its attraction on a large number of Italian women writers, some of whom adopt a strictly historical and documented approach to their writing about their country's ancient and complex civilization, while others choose to costume the historical figures that take their fancy in a narrative fictional style. Whether history or fiction, the biographies and novels about men and women alike are presented from a woman's point of view, with that woman's sense of the rhythm and cyclicality of history intuited by the late Barbara Tuchman.[1] Characters are analyzed from *within* by women authors who, from their contemporary vantage point, wonder how the figures of the past must have felt beneath their politico-social masks, their conspicuous jewelry, and their exaggerated refinery. The reader learns of the hopes, illusions, desires, and disappointments of feminine figures in Italian history, as seen by sensitive women who rewrite events of the past, and who inject into their studies those feelings of humiliation, stubborn silence, or open rebellion, which they know must have been experienced by their chosen characters.

Perhaps the best known Italian woman writer of nonfictionalized history is **Lidia Storoni Mazzolani** (1911-   ), who contributes extensively in the field of historical criticism to Italy's best newspapers (notably *La Stampa* and *La Repubblica*). Winner of the 1967 Viareggio Prize for *L'idea di città nel mondo romano* (The concept of the city in the Roman world), her volumes include *Sul mare della vita* (On the sea of life, 1969), in which she draws an interesting parallel between pagan and Christian life; *L'impero senza fine* (Unending empire, 1972), essentially a search, through her rereadings of Sallust, Livy, Tacitus, and other Roman historians, for a "reason" in history, summing up in a brilliant illustration of how the ancient world tenaciously survives in today's civilization (such as certain agrarian practices, city planning concepts, feasts, etc.); *Iscrizioni funerarie, pronostici e sortilegi di Roma antica* (Funeral inscriptions, prognostics and sorcery in ancient Rome, 1973); *La vita di Galla Placidia* (The life of Gallia Placidia, 1975), a pen portrait of the wife of the fifth Roman emperor Constantius III and mother of emperor Valentinian III. All of the aforementioned works are the fruits of lengthy documentation and deep study of crisis in the ancient Roman world. *Profili omerici* (Homeric profiles, 1978), instead, presents figures of the *Iliad* and the *Odyssey* as archetypes of human emotions and sentiments, while *Tiberio o la spirale del potere* (Tiberius or the power spiral, 1981) is an outstanding biography of Tiberius Claudius Nero Caesar, Roman emperor from 14 to 37 A.D., which studies the period extending from tribunician to imperial power. Storoni's merit is to have shown so clearly in her works how knowledge and study of the past can serve not only as a form of escape or enjoyment, but also to enrich one's inner life and develop one's critical sense— an especially important process for Italian women, who tend to assign critical judgment to the bailiwick of the male.

Also explorative of the ancient world, but in a completely different and fictionalized vein, **Maria Teresa Giuffré**'s haunting *La veglia di Adrasto* (Adrastus's watch, 1986) deserves mention. A sort of diary of nocturnal meditations by Adrastus, the second-century keeper of the Antonine column in Rome, the book is a recording of his soliloquies and colloquies with Marcus Aurelius, which reveal the bio-psychological fusion between the two (Adrastus = Marcus Aurelius's *anima*, Marcus Aurelius = the literary and historical projection of the masculine *animus*).[2] With solid grounding and expert narrative skill, Giuffré leads the historical character to interpenetrate with the narrating "I" that relates in atemporal sequences Marcus Aurelius's memoirs, bringing to them the same philosophical and speculative reflections as Storoni's on the cyclicality of human events.

Two women historians who provide the reader, through their various works on Italian historical figures, easy entry and ready approach to the two most famous historical novelists on the Italian literary scene (Maria Bellonci and Anna Banti) are **Donata Chiomenti Vassalli**, author of *Giovanna d'Aragona. Tra Baroni prìncipi e sovrani del Rinascimento* (Joan of Aragon.

Amidst barons, princes, and sovereigns of the Renaissance, 1986); *I fratelli Verri* (The Verri brothers, 1960), about the two gifted eighteenth-century Italian men of letters; *Donna Olimpia, o Del nepotismo nel Seicento* (Donna Olimpia, or On nepotism in the seventeenth century, 1979); *Giulia Beccaria, la madre del Manzoni* (Giulia Beccaria, Manzoni's mother, 1956); and **Mariana Frigeri**, author of *Ludovico il Moro. Un gentiluomo in nero* (Ludovico the Moor. A gentleman in black, 1980) and *Il Condottiero. Vita, avventure e battaglie di Bartolomeo Colleoni* (The condottiere. Life, adventures, and battles of Bartolomeo Colleoni, 1985) about the fifteenth-century Italian captain credited with being the first to develop a true field artillery tactic and who has been immortalized in Andrea del Verrocchio's superb equestrian statue standing in Campo SS. Giovanni e Paolo in Venice.

Equally well known in the rest of Europe as she is in Italy (at least two of her works are considered classics by Italian as well as foreign critics), the fame of **Maria Bellonci** (1902-1986) rests not only on her brilliant narrations but also on her founding, together with her husband and others, of a literary salon in Rome and of the Strega Prize in 1947 (see Chapter One, above).

So exact are Bellonci's biographical portraits, so well documented are her studies—replete with notes, letters, papal briefs and incunabila—and so thoroughly does she exploit Vatican library sources and Italian state archives, that it is difficult to refer to her historical narratives as "novels." Nor are they biographies: "My way of understanding History," she declared in 1973; "is not by writing biographies. I draw data from past centuries . . . and I construct. Imagination is nourished by History and History by imagination."[3]

She is a researcher with "magic intuition," who delves deeply into historical sources in order to reconstruct a documented narration in the rigorous perspective of real events. From her father, a scholar and professor of analytical chemistry, she inherited her faculty for introspection and the consideration of events from a realistic point of view, even though her poetic vision of the character she is constructing seems to be floating in an atmosphere of rarefied emotions. From her husband, Bellonci acquired an esthetic enjoyment of classical literature and from him she learned formal exercises designed to refine the flavor and quality of writing.

Bellonci's works, *Lucrezia Borgia* (*The Life and Times of Lucrezia Borgia*, 1939),[4] *Segreti dei Gonzaga* (*A Prince of Mantua:*

The Life and Times of Vincenzo Gonzaga, 1947), *Milano Viscontea* (Viscounty Milan, 1956), and *Rinascimento privato* (Private Renaissance, 1985, see Chapter Five, below), as well as two short stories contained in *Tu vipera gentile* (Thou gentle viper, 1972), one of which deals with fifteenth-century Mantua and the other with one hundred seventy years of Visconti rule in medieval and early Renaissance Milan, together form an epic narrative on Italian Renaissance courts and are variations on the theme of power and political ambition.

Bellonci's technique is to choose a historical figure from the past, "revisit" him/her from the inside, attributing the author's own sentiments, feelings, emotions, and moods to these illustrious or notorious personages. Her stated aim is to "relate, by bearing witness to them, the hopes and anguish of man and woman of all times and of all countries, impersonated in men and women of one time in one century."[5] Yet, although she enters into the world of her characters and their truths become hers, her enlightened, clinical, twentieth-century eye scrutinizes and judges the events taking place in the light of modern knowledge and practices. Lucrezia Borgia's jaundice, for example, during a difficult pregnancy, cannot be cured, declares the Duke of Este's personal physician, until after delivery—to the wonderment of Maria Bellonci who comments wryly: " . . . the violent crises that assailed her almost every day were . . . difficult to cure due to her delicate condition and her womanly nature (this last reason is mysterious)" (292). In the short story, "Soccorso a Dorotea" (Help for Dorotea), in *Tu vipera gentile,* Dorotea Gonzaga, a "child of her century," learns through crushing humiliation at the hands of Galeazzo Sforza that a woman is not "a human being born free" (146), while Isabella Fieschi, Luchino Visconti's third wife, "of that delicate and authoritative beauty typical of Ligurian women; a woman courageous in love, passionate for life in love; naturally, a rebel" (208), would have been burned at the stake by her vengeful husband's decree had he not died beforehand. Thus, Bellonci demonstrates objectively the wrongs inflicted on women in the past. In her broad messages of general truth and fundamental principles, usually contained in parenthetical phrases or concise maxims of universal verity, she boldly sweeps humanity and historical time forward in a five-century leap from the Renaissance to the twentieth century. The mental cruelty inflicted on Dorotea Gonzaga under the barbaric system of conjugal alliances to serve political ambition would not be possible today, nor would a spine curvature be sufficient reason to banish a woman to a nunnery. Nor would any contemporary ruler attempt to have himself piously buried in three places, as did Giangaleazzo Visconti who, like the snake on his family standard, sloughed off various sections of his body for placement in three different tombs (264-65). Armed patrols roaming the streets of thirteenth-century Milan under Visconti rule to break up any citizens' meetings are no different, however, from those Maria Bellonci knew under fascism in Italy: "Such police measures, as we all know, proclaim hard times for the one who is in command" (177). Not dissimilar to contemporary palmgreasing of persons in power, obtaining of favors in the late thirteenth century from the Holy Roman Emperors was best achieved by "gifts" rather than "petitions" (180-81). Commenting on the historical error of Caterina Visconti in disarming only some of her enemies, Bellonci writes astutely: " . . . the awful truth is that once you start using some weapons of violence, in order not to fail, you must use all" (276), and in *Rinascimento privato*: "I realize more and more that to rule means to live in a compact spiral of words from which we try to extricate ourselves and find the straight line of discernment. . . . But . . . does true discernment really move in a straight line or does it turn and wind in crafty and even painful meanderings?" (310). When a Visconti requires the humanists of his time to write political libels and invectives against his enemies, Bellonci weightily observes: " . . . and as always when a tyrannical regime turns to its men of letters, there is no escape for them: they must bow their heads and betray themselves" (*Tu vipera gentile*, 294). Elating over her success in declining King Francis I's invitation to join him in conquered Milan, Isabella d'Este considers: "Who knows whether we humans are foolish or wise in rejoicing over a small victory when greater disasters are imminent?" (*Rinascimento privato*, 275). Deploring pitiless plundering by Charles V, she muses: "But if Rome, the first place of civilization, had been ignominiously degraded, humanity itself was becoming degraded" (457). Nor do the bridges linking past to present escape Bellonci's observation: the 1459 Mantua Diet presided over by Pope Pius II to plan the crusade against the Turks (*Tu vipera gentile*, 114) was in essence the first political encounter among European heads of state.

The novels revolving around the feminine figures of Lucrezia Borgia, Caterina Sforza, Isabella d'Este, Barbara and Dorotea Gonzaga, and others, describe the life and times, the loves and wars, the courts and cities, and the gowns and jewels of these famous ladies, but likewise paint prismatically their inner portraits, moods and memories. Bellonci has stated that in her choice of characters she is interpreting her own inner movement, that through a given character she tells about her own life, and, further, that the myth is shared by surrounding people, so that she is, for example, not only Lucrezia Borgia but also Pope Alexander VI, and her friends become other characters in the "autobiography."[6] The reader, therefore, after delving into hundreds of pages of dense Renaissance history, is invariably left with the sharp sensation that he/she has been made privy to personal sentiments and secrets that far outweigh in importance the external historical events that contain them. Even beyond personal concerns, Bellonci offers broader and deeper politico-historical reflections: whenever a city is to be "pacified" in preparation for a papal visit, the reader is invited to consider (in one of Bellonci's poniard-like parentheses that are pregnant with blame) how many suspects wound up in prison (*Tu vipera gentile*, 119). In the coeval story-within-the-story about a peasant and his lord, Bellonci reproaches the chronicler for having concluded the tale without even mentioning the swelling anguish and terror in the poor peasant who had made some terrible gaffes before learning that the stranger with whom he is speaking so familiarly is none other than his seignior, Bernabó Visconti (232). Through Bellonci's innumerable touches of sarcasm and humor, one is forced to read into Italian Renaissance history a whole gamut of human emotions, and concomitantly share the indignation and skepticism of the author.

Another extraordinary skill of Bellonci is her gentle prodding of the reader to refresh his/her memory on the artistic and literary figures of the times. She expertly interweaves the characters under study with their familiar coeval painters and poets. The play of light and dark and choice of details in certain descriptions by the seventeenth-century narrator of "Delitto di stato" (State crime) are highly evocative of Caravaggio's techniques: " . . . in that darkness of memory I discern only her hand offering me the melon: white and naked hand on the silver platter. Very clear instead is my recollection of [my following behind] the servant who was holding up a lantern" (25). Andrea Mantegna is collocated in the court of the Gonzagas where the nobles' reactions to this venerable Paduan classical artist are recorded (118), while Pollaiolo's portrait of Galeazzo Sforza hanging in the Uffizi Gallery is the basis of a stunning character analysis by Bellonci of this sadistic tyrant (151). Likewise, Pisanello's splendid medal bearing the likeness of the maniacal Filippo Maria Visconti is the springboard for Bellonci's keen analysis of the "turbid ferment of a superior intelligence" (290), while the funerary monument by Paolo Uccello in Santa Maria del Fiore of the condottiere John Hawkwood, husband of one of Bernabó Visconti's thirty-two legitimate and illegitimate children, elicits one of Maria Bellonci's pleasant persiflages. Giotto, the greatest artistic genius of the thirteenth century, having been called to Milan by the enlightened ruler, Azzore Visconti, to decorate parts of the palace, is evoked in his glorious artistic creation that parallels Plutarch's *Lives* (200).

Explaining the circumstances of poetry and prose of the times, Bellonci recalls that famous poets were born or lived in some of the places where historical events are occurring. The reader is caught up in her associations of Vergil's birthplace near Mantua (the setting for "Soccorso a Dorotea") and his influence on the Renaissance humanists. In several pages of *Tu vipera gentile*, "maestro Dante Alighieri" moves to and from between Florence and Milan; Beatrice d'Este, with her first husband, Nino di Gallura, a friend of Dante, find their place in *The Divine Comedy* (181-82), after which Petrarch appears writing sonnets of circumstance in Milan, while his friend, Boccaccio, urges him to return to Florence. Moreover, the form of government that had been conceived in fourteenth-century Visconti Milan gives a foretaste, Bellonci reminds the reader, of Niccoló Macchiavelli's thought in *The Prince*. Pietro Bembo's unsuccessful courting of Lucrezia Borgia in Ferrara is evoked sympathetically and detailedly by Bellonci, as is Ludovico Ariosto's flame for the Florentine lady, Alessandra Benucci, but it is reprovingly that she uses information on the courtesan "Fiammetta" supplied by Pietro Aretino "in one of the less clean pages of his filthy 'Dialogues'" (*Lucrezia Borgia*, 157).

Maria Bellonci's novels proceed at a vital pace, relentlessly involving the reader in an underlying suspicion of the instruments of power, and swinging from an almost occasional approach to human affairs to the deep permanency of historical occurrences. Juxtaposed history and narrative, imagination and sensitivity, warmth and creativity, render her books unique in their genre. Her notable success as an historical novelist is truly deserved, and her Lucrezia Borgia has come to symbolize the learned woman who dared to affirm her own personality, vindicate her right to live autonomously, and pursue her own objectives of happiness and glory, even at the desperately high and deeply dramatic price of posterity's associating her, with her father and brother, in extremes of iniquity.

The hallmark of the elaborately articulated historical novels of **Anna Banti** (pseudonym of Lucia Lopresti Longhi, 1895-1985) is the complex relationship between history and the feminine character. Banti is moved to write through her contemplation of the painful solitude of the modern women desiring to engage in a free and original activity but faced with the challenges of a society that has invented innumerable pretexts to deny her the time, space, and other requirements for the development of her talent. (The themes of degradation, male specular vision, and dependency are treated also by art critic **Marisa Volpi**, a pupil of Banti's husband, Roberto Longhi, in her collection of short stories, *Maestro della betulla* [The birch tree painter, 1986]).

Novelist, short-story writer, biographer, and critic,[7] as well as translator of Virginia Woolf, Anna Banti's university studies were in the field of art history—which has considerably colored her writing. Bringing to her works mystery, imagination, atmosphere, and internally reflected facial expression and postures in a painterly way, she earned praise from critics Bernard Berenson and Sir Harold Acton. Similar to Bellonci, whose husband was a distinguished literary critic, Banti was married, as has been noted, to a prominent art historian, and she herself loved to delve into archives in search of dusty documents whose faded ink characters enchanted and inspired her.

Banti engaged in varied, intense writing and research activities, publishing as well several books on the theme of the low status and sense of isolation of the intelligent Italian woman. But she devoted herself principally to historical prose, in which past and present mingle and overlap, reminding the reader once again that time and history are nothing but the eternal present, and that historical figures are our own contemporaries. In her historically constructed *La camicia bruciata* (The burned night-robe, 1973), the protagonists, Princesses Marguerite and Violante, unhappily married to the father and son, respectively, of the last Medici princes, seem to be dialoguing with the author as though they were still alive,[8] while in *Artemisia* (1947), Banti uses the realistic tones and chiaroscuro colors of Caravaggio (whom she considered absolute Master in art) as the poetic substance of her historical novel. In evoking Marguerite's, Violante's, and Artemisia's dramatic psychological lacerations and painful solitude, Banti's own feelings and reactions are mingled with those of her characters, all of whom claim, by their words, thoughts, or acts, the right to social equality and spiritual and cultural parity between the sexes. The author refers only marginally to the polemical points of the feminist movement, giving importance instead to the inner, spiritual needs of modern women—symbols, for Banti, of a human condition that must be defined and defended against obsolete conventions.[9] Thus, in writing her historical novels, Banti recruits heroines for the ranks of supporters of the equality of the sexes, and treats the episodes of their lives not only in form of historical narration but as a vehicle for intimating her own endurance of impediments, inhibitions, and frustrations in her writing career. Princess Marguerite Louise d'Orléans in *La camicia bruciata*, an illustrious victim of injustice and hypocrisy in a seventeenth-century society in which women are "always wrong" (141) and, "as is well known, negligible objects that Courts exchange as necessary instruments for obtaining offspring" (207), set fire to her wedding night-robe (hence the title of the novel) as a gesture of protest against her arranged political marriage to Cosimo III de' Medici. Although she had accepted the wish of her sovereign, King Louis XIV of France, that she unite in wedlock with the prince of Tuscany, before the marriage she exercised her woman's prerogative of changing her mind because, languid, romantic heroine that she was, she thought she was in love with her cousin, Charles of Lorraine. Seeking desperately to extricate herself from her promise, Marguerite requested a second audience with her King: she "prostrates herself, tearfully kisses the hand of Europe's most feared monarch, who icily responds: 'You should have thought of that earlier, my honor is engaged, either Tuscany or the convent'" (21). Forced to submit, Marguerite is so miserable in Florence, and finds it so impossible to love her husband, that she lets all of France know that she would not have been unhappier if she had been miserably wed "in the humblest hut in France" (74). After the birth of her three children, and years of frosty, bitter exchanges with her husband and the closed Florentine court (which admirably illustrate age-old French/Italian rivalries), Marguerite finally makes her escape into the mournful convent of Montmartre in Paris, without, however, having succeeded in obtaining the annulment of her marriage, since Cosimo's offspring required legitimacy for Medicean political purposes. After years of scandalous behavior in and outside the convent, frenetic but egoistic dedication to the sick and suffering, and other diversionary tactics, Marguerite is finally readmitted to Luxembourg Palace, where, now aged and

decrepit, she is practically forgotten by all. In Florence, meanwhile, her bizarre younger son, Gastone, converses secretly with
the palace portraits of his mother, while her dissolute elder son,
Cosimo's heir, Ferdinando, enters into marriage with Beatrice
Violante of Bavaria, a plain but polite, docile, devoted princess—
just the opposite of Marguerite—who communicates with the
ghost of her absent mother-in-law. As though deriving strength
and protection from Marguerite, Violante withstands the decline
and fall of the Medicean dynasty, but after the death of Ferdinando, suddenly becomes possessed of all the qualities that constitute Anna Banti's own ideals: quickness and combativeness,
easy rousing against injustice and tyranny, and repugnance for
fanaticism. Rather than return to Bavaria, as is expected, Violante succeeds in setting up a small court in her widow's country villa (Lappeggi, near Florence)—a sort of Arcadia where
painters, musicians, and poets exercise their arts in her gracious
presence. Finally, by unanimous vote of the Florentine Council,
she is named Governor of Siena, where she will represent the
Grand Duke's authority in the Tuscan city. Enlightened,
clement, benevolent, and indulgent, scrupulous in her administration of the city's budget and refusing ever to sign a death
penalty, Violante brings wisdom and gentleness to her rule.
Never had Siena been so peaceful; never had the city flourished
as during her governorship. It is Violante who, in the end, will
rehabilitate the "ghost" of Marguerite and restore some dignity
to the figure that Cosimo de' Medici, with implacable rancor,
had shamed, condemned, and driven out of Florence.

In *La camicia bruciata*, Banti, with irony, reason, and fantasy, intimates that the two women, Marguerite and Violante,
would fit nicely into our own century. The reader comes away
from the novel with a feeling of feminine solidarity with these
two seventeenth-century princesses, for whom time, "nailed in
place" at certain significant events (117), is "an instant that seems
to last a century" (59).

The anticonformist seventeenth-century artist, Artemisia
Gentileschi (1597-after 1651), daughter of the famous Orazio Gentileschi included by Van Dyck in his portraits of a hundred illustrious men, painted in Italian milieux hostile to women artists;
nevertheless she succeeded in obtaining commissions from the
Florentine court, establishing an art school in Naples, and receiving an invitation to paint at the heretical Court of England.
She gained renown, even greater than her father's, for her
baroque portrait paintings, yet she always received lower

stipends "because she [was] a woman." In *Artemisia*, a novel
that is a perfect example of highly refined erudition, Banti in-
vokes her heroine from an unusual vantage point: the Boboli
gardens, filled with an exodus of refugees escaping Florence
(Banti's birthplace) under destruction by German mines during
World War II. The manuscript of the original *Artemisia*, written in the form of a short story, had been lost during the war.
Stubbornly, Banti reconstructs her work and rewrites it in the
form of an open diary, so that the final version is the result of a
double search: for what had been lost, and for a dialogue with
Artemisia. Weeping over the loss of her incompleted
manuscript, Banti hears a gentle voice at her side (evocative of
the dialogue between Violante and Marguerite in *La camicia
bruciata*) begging her to bring the heroine to life once again in
the author's memory that had been shattered by the outbreak of
the war, and urging her to resume their common recollections
of the city of Florence. As the novel progresses, whenever the
author becomes still, deciding that she will no longer allow
Artemisia to speak and that she will no longer speak for her because "in my present there no longer is any place for the past nor
for the future" (28), a small, obstinate, querulous voice goads her
to get on with the narrative. When the author threatens to
leave Florence permanently, Artemisia spitefully "upsets an entire pot of ink onto the page" and then they "look at each other
sympathetically" (121). It is this gentle banter between the two
women that gives the book its flash back-and-forward rhythm
and seems to be the instrument that measures Anna Banti's te-
lescoped time.

Biographical sources up to recent years reported that
Artemisia "refused" a marriage offer from Agostino Tasso, a
landscape painter associated with her father, and "chose" to
marry Pier Antonio Schiattesi, a petty merchant. Banti's documented reality is that the thirteen-year-old Artemisia, having
been raped by Agostino Tasso, courageously denounced him,
only to be further humiliated by his offer to marry her if she
would sign a statement that he was "not the first." Forced into a
hastily arranged marriage with the unloved Schiattesi in order
to be worthy of a place in society and protection as her father's
pupil, Artemisia plays out the tragedy of a gifted girl subjected to
absurd social rules and regulations. Living a widow's existence,
far from her merchant husband who will later request dissolution of their bond in order to marry a native girl from the West
Indies, Artemisia devotes herself exclusively to her career as an

artist, remaining firm in her intimate need to create, even at the price of impopularity and loneliness.

Banti's style is tight, intricate, sometimes declamatory, sometimes conversational, rich in epigrammatic expressions, and always strict in its infallible choice of the *mot juste*. Her inverted subject-object sequences, and highly varied syntax conforming to the Latinity of the Italian language, lend the novel the flavor of *secentismo* (Italian baroque) as well as a tinge of the heroic epic. Travelling alone on an ill-equipped ship described in startling onomatopœias and other figures of speech, the lonely Artemisia peers out into her dark future: " . . . the lighthouse had disappeared, black was the sea . . . " (195). "A woman who would like to be a man in order to escape herself" (140), Artemisia is at the same time a very modern figure suffering an existential "repugnance for life, a nausea that becomes physical" (182), even though the sea on which she sails is perfectly calm.

Banti's message in these works and elsewhere is clear: woman is permitted freely to procreate but not to create. If she has creative talent, either she must keep it secret, as though it were blameworthy (the theme of one of her short stories, "Lavinia fuggita" [Runaway Lavinia, 1963], relating the struggle of a woman composer); or she must accept the woman-artist's punishment (as in *Artemisia*); or she must defy and scandalize society (as in *La camicia bruciata* and the more modern *Il bastardo*, a novel about a woman who shocks her entourage by becoming an electrical engineer and workshop foreman). The tone and intent of these works give a foretaste of a fiercely feminist book, *Allarme sul lago* (Alarm on the lake, 1954), in which Banti unleashes expressions of contemptuous pity against the male.

Women are notably absent, however, from Banti's 1967 historical novel, *Noi credevamo* (We believed, 1967), based on the memoirs of her grandfather, whose life spanned one of Italy's most historical periods: ca. 1809-1883. The story is set in the Risorgimento and post-Risorgimento years, and is told, in the first person singular, by the Calabrian patriot, Domenico Lopresti. Having endured imprisonment for his subversive activities under the Bourbon kings of Naples, Lopresti then suffered defeat and disillusionment as he passed from the heroic ranks of Garibaldi's followers in the struggle for republican national unity, to the lowly grade of state employee in the service of the Italian monarchy. Sir Harold Acton wrote, concerning *Noi credevamo*, that it was "a profound parable for the young Communist intellectuals of today [1967], doomed to disillusion, frustration and despair. As such it seemed to me courageous and original, a novel of unusual value."[10] More generally, *Noi credevamo* may be viewed as a symbolic novel, in which Anna Banti conveys both a personal and a universal sense of melancholy and dissatisfaction affecting men and women alike, of all political parties, under all forms of government, and in all walks of life. Perhaps Banti's frame of mind at the time of her writing *Noi credevamo* was analogous to the spirit of an almost contemporaneous piece of art work hanging in the Peggy Guggenheim Collection in Venice: Mark Tobey's gouache and watercolor on paper entitled "Advance of History" (1964). It consists of nothing more than many crossing lines that seem to be going in no direction whatsoever; yet a few bold, underlying strokes reassure the viewer that there *must* be a path along which history advances.

"Dust returneth to dust again," **Rosetta Loy** (1931-   ) reminds the reader in each chapter of her saga, *Le strade di polvere* (Dusty roads, 1987).[11] The novel's setting is Monferrato, the muddy, snowy, foggy Piedmont massif near Turin, whose easternmost town, Casale Monferrato, was an important stronghold under the Gonzagas of Mantua. The historical time of Loy's novel, however, is not the Mantuan Renaissance described by Bellonci but rather the era of the dust-laden, muffled whirlwind moving across nineteenth-century Italy: the Napoleonic invasions and the wars of independence against Austria. In muted brown, white, and gray tones, the vicissitudes of a closely knit, patriarchal farming family are described against a distant backdrop of French troops in Italy under Napoleon, Austrian predominance in northern Italy after 1815, the unsuccessful nationalist insurrections of 1820, 1831, and 1848, and the role of Piedmont, under the impelling force of Victor Emanuel II and Cavour, in achieving the unification of Italy (1859-1870). Although related in a somewhat romantic, fable-like style, the physical and emotional hardships endured by the Monferrato family are real and cruel. Consumed clothing that scarcely keeps out the cold, widespread contagious conjunctivitis, cholera attacks and natural catastrophes are evoked by the author but toned down and softened by folkish superstitions and ineluctable passions, which give rise to comforting mysterious signs and presences.

After sharing in the joys and sorrows, feasts and tragedies, weddings and deaths of three generations of the "Gran Masten" family, the reader is left, in the large home surrounded by apple trees, cornfields, and vineyards, alone with the old folk who are "closed in an impassable circle of silence" (240) in the twilight of an era. The only possible words that remain to be uttered are "It's time to go to sleep"—words that seem to have the force of wind blowing through the darkened house, raising dust from the old furniture and causing the house to creak and squeak like a ship at roadstead.

A biography of the turn-of-the-century femme fatale, Russian Countess Maria Tarnovska, is **Donatella Pecci Blunt's** *La contessa in rosso* (The countess in red, 1989). The beautiful, cultured countess in question had been sentenced to prison by a Venetian court in 1910 for complicity in the murder of her lover—the story that Annie Vivanti had treated in her 1912 novel entitled *Circe*. Tarnovska, amnestied in 1915, fell into a life of dissolution and died in Argentina in 1949 at the age of seventy-two. Her story is told through the eyes of her son, against a backdrop of the decadent atmosphere of the end of Europe's "belle époque." Author Pecci Blunt wanders from the documented biography, however, preferring to imagine Maria Tarnovska coming to grips with her betrayed aspirations and her disenchantment with matrimony.

Five sentimental historical episodes of the eighteenth, nineteenth, and twentieth centuries form **Gina Lagorio's** novel, *Tra le mura stellate* (Within the star-shaped walls, 1991, in the final running for the Strega Prize). The author allows her happy childhood memories to surface in the Piedmont setting of the town of Cherasco.

A rigorously documented biography, on the other hand, about a famous Lombardy family, is **Natalia Ginzburg's** *La famiglia Manzoni* (*The Manzoni Family*, Bagutta Prize, 1983),[12] which topples from his pedestal the nineteenth-century Italian novelist and poet, Alessandro Manzoni, famous for his historical novel, *I promessi sposi*, and presents him as a tormented, troubled, egoistic figure, as well as a failure as a father.

Saint Theresa of Lisieux is portrayed psychoanalytically in a novel, *La prima estasi* (The first ecstasy, 1985), by **Elisabetta Rasy**, cofounder of one of the first publishing houses for women in Italy; **Mimi Zorzi's** *Il medico di famiglia* (Family physician, 1981) is the story of a Milanese family, unfolding between 1940-68; and **Graziella Civiletti's** *Il ritratto della bella fortunata* (Portrait of a lucky lady, 1981) is a saga in traditional style of a Roman family during the century 1870-1970. The outstanding resistance novel by a women writer is **Renata Viganò's** *L'Agnese* *va a morire* (Agnes goes to die, Viareggio Prize, 1949) inspired by her own experience in the partisan struggle, while **Marina Sereni**'s *I giorni della nostra vita* (The days of our life, 1955) is a personal story of the militant antifascists' struggle, in which the Communist Party is the real protagonist. **Isabella Bossi Fedrigotti**'s novel, *Casa di guerra* (House of war, 1983) takes place in the World War II spring of 1944 in the Trentino region, still plagued by confusion both in the political entity of the South Tyrol and in the souls of its people, torn between the Austrians and the Italians.

The mid-twentieth-century tragedy of all of Italy is vividly and poignantly captured by **Elsa Morante** and **Natalia Ginzburg**, the former in *History: A Novel* (1974), a neorealistic epic of the endless terror of war and of the tragedy that befell Italy because of Mussolini's and Hitler's follies; the latter in *Tutti i nostri ieri* (*All Our Yesterdays*, 1952), a long novel about fascism and the war years.

Whereas Morante's *Arturo's Island* (Chapter Two, above) was clearly a nonhistorical, mythical work, *History: A Novel*, reflected on and written during 1971-74, is a representative, historical novel on World War II and is generally considered a major contribution to modern Italian literature. Just as Morante's supporters and denigrators in literary and political circles took diametrically different positions regarding this work, likewise in the novel, in stark opposition, stand the humble and pure of heart vs. the powerful who unleash wars and persecutions. Morante's purpose in writing the book was in fact to set in contrast the ineluctable unpreparedness of humble people vis-à-vis the deadly machine by which they are triturated.

The novel covers a progression of disasters in the lives of its fictional characters during Europe's conflagration as well as during the pre-war period of fascism. It shows Italy at its worst, in its mediocrity, a tiny power trying to create an "empire," ravaged by war, then prostrate in the postwar period. Mixed components of history and invention give the novel its impact: the reader is inexorably involved in the clash between the dark, destructive forces of History, and the affairs of its human protagonists—in this case, the simple schoolteacher, Ida Ramundo, and her little boy, Giuseppe. Intentionally and purposefully does the author write History with a capital H, as does the contemporary French writer, Georges Perec, who has declared that he has no childhood memories, all of them having been lopped off by History—"l'Histoire avec sa grande hache" (in French, the letter *h* is pronounced like the word "hache" meaning axe, so the significance is: History with a capital H, or History with its big axe).[13]

Morante's unpretentious characters try desperately to expel this frighteningly powerful force from their private, personal lives; it is an incomprehensible evil they refuse to accept; they look with horror on the savagery of both the German invaders of Europe and the partisans who sought to expel them, and on the senseless and barbarous racial persecutions, illustrated in the novel by moving descriptions, through a child's eyes, of trains loaded with humble Italian Jewish deportees leaving Rome's Tiburtina station, and the bustling ghetto reduced to a deserted ghost neighborhood.

The main action takes place in Rome between 1941 and 1947. There appear to be two Narrators: an objective third person who formulates chronologies, and a subjective "I" who relates personally to the characters. Ida Ramundo, the frail, shabby, uncomprehending daughter of a Jewish mother (whom the Italian racial laws of 1938 apparently drove to suicide) and a Calabrian non-Jewish father, who is an anarchist and an alcoholic, suffered, as a child, from petit mal. After her marriage to the Sicilian, Alfio, the couple moves to Rome, where Ida does all in her power to cling to bourgeois propriety, but she belongs, fatally, to Morante's realm of the downtrodden and the oppressed. Alfio has died of cancer before the story begins, leaving Ida with a son, Nino—an exuberant, defiant, undisciplined lad who had left school, become a partisan, passed the German lines to go South, whence he reappears in Rome deeply involved in the black market. Ida imagines the rambunctious Nino as an invulnerable superman, much in the same way as Arturo idolized and idealized his father, Wilhelm Gerace. Following serious injury in a road accident caused by his illicit trade, Nino meets an early death—one of Morante's many demonstrations that History and the war are indirectly responsible for senseless loss of life.

When Nino was still in his teens, Ida was raped by a drunken German soldier of the occupying forces in Rome who came from Dachau—the very town that was to provide History with sixty-six thousand victims, making the outrageous violation of Ida, by comparison, pitifully unimportant. The visionary, poetic, mystic, epileptic child born of the injurious union, Giuseppe, spends the few years of his life in a state of utter innocence and felicity, despite the forms of violence History forces him to witness: air raids, evacuees indecorously packed into ill-smelling shanties, deportations, photographs of concentration camp victims. Giuseppe's own personal nightmares give expression to the deep psychological traumas he suffers, and in vain does his mother attempt to construct a figurative golden cage to protect him and the birds whose songs Giuseppe sings. The portrayal of the flimsy little boy is so touching that even Stephen Spender, who found much to criticize in the novel, wrote that "Elsa Morante sees children in the light of their pathos . . . and in its way the portrait of Giuseppe is the most inspired invention in this book."[14]

After a bombing of Rome in which most of her building is destroyed, Ida is forced to move with Giuseppe to a crude shelter on the outskirts of Rome that houses innumerable colorful families (all sympathetically described by Morante, but especially the proliferative Neapolitans). Giuseppe is the poorest child of all in the shelter, where semblances of decency and privacy are hard to preserve, where winter and the cold bring illness, lack of hygiene brings rats and cockroaches, and promiscuity brings degradation. When, finally, Ida is able to obtain a small room with use of a kitchen in the slum area near the school where she teaches, the tiny space seems a luxurious domain to her. Continuing indomitably her struggle against hunger and the difficulties caused by war, whose end remains elusive, Ida suffers extreme privation herself but succeeds in providing for Giuseppe's needs. Morante's moving portrait of the cold and hungry schoolteacher facing each winter of war in Rome, is unsurpassed: Ida teaches, cares for her epileptic son, gives private lessons to earn extra money, markets, cooks, cleans, corrects her pupils' homework, and eats whatever leftovers she finds. No relatives, no friends, no visitors ever cross her threshold; the solitary Ida is forced to guard her two secrets (her non-Aryan mother and the illegitimacy of Giuseppe) lest she lose her teaching position. Drained of vitality and of teaching effectiveness, improperly dressed, fatigued and somnolent, Ida becomes the laughing stock of her pupils. She is incapable, however, of punishing them even though they now appear to her clouded vision as spiteful and malicious dwarfs.

Despite her deterioration, Ida retains an extraordinary poetic quality: poor in spirit and victim of atrociously overwhelming experiences, she is nevertheless full of grace and altruism. Uncomplaining, encouraging others to live, she represents Life standing and fighting against blind History—until the day she returns from school to find Giuseppe dead as the result of repeated epileptic attacks. No longer does Ida desire to belong to the human species: whining like an animal, she falls into a deep insanity that lasts nine vegetative years until her demise. But those nine years, concludes the Narrator, were only a pulsation for her: in reality she died when Giuseppe did.

A secondary character in the novel, who serves to air Elsa Morante's political views, is Nino's friend, Davide Segre, who is also doomed to destruction by History. A deeply convinced humanist and anarchist, in revolt against his bourgeois forebears, the tormented Davide lives out a personal tragedy of loss of faith, drug addiction, inevitable degradation, and self-destruction. Of Dostoyevskian matrix, Davide is the most literary and dramatically suffering character of the story. He would like to be pacific in opposition to endless fascist violence, but as a wartime partisan he becomes cruel and ruthless. The reasoning that permeates his thought is that his social class, the bourgeoisie, must be crushed, but a few days' work in a factory as a manual laborer to become part of the proletariat is a disastrous baptism of fire for him. Davide expresses hatred and horror of drugs (then considered a bourgeois vice), but ends up their easy victim. His lacerations and traumas being the result of the clash between his convictions and the reality of life, Davide Segre is the desperate witness of an ideological failure and, as such, expresses the despairing and funereal side of Elsa Morante herself.

An extrapolation of the world's principal political misdeeds and crimes immediately contemporaneous with the corresponding period in the lives of Ida, Nino, Giuseppe, and Davide prefaces each year in the novel's action. Thus, the characters are virtually imprisoned within the first and last chapters of the book, both labeled 19**, a duplication that once again gives emphasis to the circular, cyclical, and rhythmic nature of History— Morante's synonym for Hecatomb. The author has purposely taken this peculiar approach to her tale to bring history and narrative into confrontation, and to give a *whole* response to the reality and significance of world events. The historicity of her novel lends truth to the fictional lie.

The concluding chronology of the 1950s and 1960s is a succession of bloody and threatening events, followed by the simple phrase: " . . . and History continues . . . ," implying that an inexorable force will always corrupt oppressors and victims alike, and that the beauties of this planet and humankind's happiness will forever be destroyed by public and private slaughter. So

devastated is Morante by the "scandal that started ten thousand
years ago" and by the ugliness of our atomic century, it is no
wonder that she preferred the "magic novel" that insists on the
fable and on the redemptive world of childhood. She is inclined
to believe that the world's only salvation is in little children (cf.
her collection of poetry, *Il mondo salvato dai ragazzini*,[15] as well
as an entire corpus of post-World War II literature in Italy and
elsewhere in which children figure extensively as a redemptive
force). For Elsa Morante, as for Marguerite Duras, women have
an exceptional capacity for listening, and it is they who hear with
thoughtful attention the sounds uttered by children. Children,
in their turn, are alert to catch the tones of nature and seem able
to transform gray reality into joyful visual and auditory experiences, causing the world to appear like a shining garden devoid
of sadness or ugliness. Children are perhaps the "seed" Morante
refers to on the penultimate page of the novel, after her recognition of the bitter fact that "History continues": on the final, clean
white page of her book, which contrasts meaningfully with the
densely printed blackness of the preceding pages, are engraved
the words of an Italian political prisoner of fascism which invite
the reader to keep hope alive:

> All the seeds failed, except one. I don't know what it
> is, but it is probably a flower and not a weed.

A book without dialogue, narrated in the third person in
indirect discourse, **Natalia Ginzburg**'s (1916-1991) *All Our Yesterdays*, 1952 (also translated as *Dead Yesterdays* and as *A Light
for Fools*) is a novel of ambitious scope. It tells the story of a
generation living out moments of poignant sorrow during the
antifascist struggle and Italy's war for liberation, in a narrative
movement that takes the reader from an unidentified northern
industrial town to a village in southern Italy. The events are
parallelled by a gradual altering and upsetting of bourgeois complacency that ends in a growing accumulation of violence associated with the experience of war.

Two bourgeois families live in houses fronting each
other. In one lives a lawyer—a widower—who is waging singlehanded and obstinately a battle against the fascist dictatorship,
using as his weapon his book of antifascist memoirs (which,
however, will never see the light of publication). His children,
Anna, Concettina, Ippolito, and Giustino, more or less victims of
their authoritarian but erratic parent, are adolescents forcefully
and penetratingly portrayed by Ginzburg.[16] His father's amanu-

ensis, the pale Ippolito takes dictation or reads Goethe aloud, while the frivolous Concettina, unconnected with and alienated from the rest of her family, flits from one to the other of her various boyfriends. Ippolito will be the first victim in the novel: the day after Italy's entry in the war, he is found dead on a park bench—a depressive suicide despairing at the military preponderance of the Germans. A similar but more heroic victim will be the German Jew, Franz, who is involved in a sentimental relationship with the young, snobbish wife of the wealthy industrialist who lives with his family in the second bourgeois household. The children in this well-to-do family unit are a daughter, Amalia, and two boys, Emanuele and Giuma.

Both heads of family die shortly after the opening of the novel, allowing the continuation of the plot to develop around the relationships struck up among themselves by the children in both homes. Anna, the lawyer's plain and insecure daughter, becomes bizarrely and perversely involved with the spoiled adolescent, Giuma. She becomes pregnant and is generously accepted as a wife by Cenzo Rena, a mature friend of the family, despite the great difference in their ages. After the wedding, Anna and Cenzo go to live in his southern village of Borgo San Costanzo, where the realities of World War II are felt through their repercussions in the peasant world:[17] lack of basic needs, men continuously leaving for the front, the arrival in town of large numbers of prisoners, mostly Jews. Just before the end of the war, the politically motivated Cenzo sacrifices his life to save lives threatened by the Germans, and Franz, in a gesture of solidarity, likewise offers his chest to the executionary bullets fired in the public square of Borgo San Costanzo, in a sacrificial rite symbolizing the bold contribution of heroes and martyrs to the cause of justice and the redemption of mankind. Anna, returning with her child to her native town, is reunited with those family members and friends that have survived the conflict. She and her brother, Giustino, together will face their uncertain future, with nothing left to them save the bitter sweetness of knowing and feeling that they are alive.

Thus, Ginzburg's realistic novel sinks its roots into existential anguish. Her women characters are desperately alone, and the ambiance and characters she describes sometimes seem to exhale an odor of staleness, as though they were wrapped in an impalpable cover of dust and mold. This should not, however, mislead the reader, for the author's apparent negativity takes a certain positive turn, sometimes ironic, but she permits her characters to stand up against destruction and decay, especially on the plane of morality and sentiments.

The spiritual disorientation that followed the euphoria of the immediate postwar period in Italy is transmitted to the reader through the vicissitudes of Anna's life: her youth, spent in building empty castles in the air; her precocious motherhood in adolescence; her marriage of convenience to a family friend; her loss of family members; and the living out of a dismal, portentous destiny as she searches for values to which she can conform her vision of the world. With pondered cautiousness, Ginzburg overtly expresses her hope that the harsh experiences of all our yesterdays may help illuminate and presage a less uncertain future for the generations of tomorrow. The novel remains pessimistic, however. Even though History is not presented in Elsa Morante's apocalyptic tones, nevertheless the historical elements of Ginzburg's work provoke confusion, disorder, discomposure, clashes, and destruction, and loom large until they fill the entire space of each day, just as in Ginzburg's novel that is most representative of the so-called "letteratura della memoria"—Lessico famigliare (Family Sayings, see Chapter Four, below). Both novels embrace a broad and highly significant timespan in Italian history; in both, however, the existential drama of all of Italy's yesterdays is played out on the stage of daily life and family relationships, and the role played by History is that of supernumerary. The events that involve the community of human beings are seen through individual reactions, personal moods, and the intimate life of family members, as well as through personalized, privatized conceptions of Mussolini, the King of Italy, and the fatherland. Both All Our Yesterdays and Family Sayings are highly evocative works in which the little groups of characters seem to take on the proportions of a historic crowd bent on distinguishing itself in responding to events during Italy's struggle to regain its freedom.

Chapter Four

The Self-recounting Novel

If the objective of historical novelists is to "*raccontare per raccontare*" (recount for the sake of recounting), in recent years the more persistent trend has been in the direction of "*raccontare per raccontarsi*" (recount in order to self-recount).[1] An increasing number of Italian women authors seemingly feel the need to turn inward, plumb their inner depths, and examine minutely and critically the sensations and emotions that spring from the changes, contradictions, and turbulence investing them. Feeling an eagerness and an urgency to narrate, women writers ostensibly are searching for an appropriate language to give expression to their inner selves and in this respect a stylistic evolution seems to be in progress. This is evident in a plethora of novels or strict autobiographies in which the authors set down on their radiographic pages, in the first person singular or through a mirror character, aspects of their own lives and their own struggle to become writers.

Encompassing forms of "confessionalism," "intimism," "re-evocation," and "flow of memory," the type of writing broadly known as "*letteratura della memoria*" (denoted in this chapter as "self-recounting literature") implies a certain narcissism and a cult of self. To wonder whether self-narration stems from a lack of modesty, or naïveté, or whether it reveals a basic insecurity on the part of the author-narrator, is, however, superfluous. What is of interest, instead, is to examine the author's selective choice—on the conscious or unconscious level—of past events, and to scrutinize her fashion of recreating time gone by. The author's recollections, usually triggered by a word, a gesture, or a "family saying," represent an effort to understand and explain present-day realities in terms of what has happened in the past. She surveys, in retrospective mood, a considerable portion of her life. The aim of this chapter is to discover whether her ideas, sentiments, emotions, concepts, struggles, and catharses can lend themselves to universal interpretation, and whether they can be channeled in some way into the reader's own life, modifying it or bettering his/her knowledge and understanding of human problems.

No longer being simply an "object of narration" (i.e. a character written about), a woman writing about herself treads on risky ground. Unless she wraps herself in protective armor against prejudices, misunderstandings, and negative criticism, she is doomed to defeat. One of the best arms for defense is, perhaps, success, which once achieved, opens the way for her to write about herself without qualms,[2] and, in fact, many autobiographical novels by women authors have turned out to be successes. As the "narrating subjects" of their works, women writers are giving expression to an obsessive *"bisogno/sogno"*[3] (the play on words in Italian is lost in the English translation "need/dream")—a concept that is best rendered as an inner necessity to concretize the vision of a new kind of writing. By projecting themselves both inwards and outwards, authors of self-recounting novels become involved in an act of supreme creativity requiring simultaneous introspection and expansion.

Numerous are the Italian women authors (especially those living in socially backward situations, for whom novels serve as a sort of vengeance[4]) who transpose, through a protagonist-narrator, their actual experience of study and reflection, and for whom writing constitutes an autobiographical creative act.

Early examples are Sibilla Aleramo's *Una donna*, published in 1906 (see Chapter Six, below), Grazia Deledda's *Cosima* (published posthumously in 1937), and *Stella mattutina* (Morning star, 1921) by Ada Negri, whose name, like Matilde Serao's, was also being considered in 1926 for the Nobel Prize but the high regard in which Mussolini held his allegedly favorite poetess may have caused the Swedish jury to balk.

The archaic fascination of both the island of Sardinia and of a small, timid woman resembling a young fawn who was to become a Nobel Prize winner are nicely wielded in **Grazia Deledda**'s autobiographical novel, *Cosima* (the author's middle name). Set in her native village of Nuoro (the scene of practically all her writings), *Cosima* should perhaps be read first, before Deledda's other works are approached, for a better grasp of the genesis of her vast literary output. The novelized diary, written in the third person singular, may be divided into two parts, the first of which carefully reconstructs Cosima's childhood in her parents' home. Here she grew up in close contact with nature and the eternal passions, jealousies, and hates of the people of Sardinia, as well as with its myths of supernatural justice, which powerfully influenced her childhood imagination. Even though Cosima did not mingle socially with the Nuorese villagers inasmuch as she was considered a *"signorina per bene"* (a well-bred young lady), she nevertheless felt at one in spirit with them. By listening closely to what they related about their lives as they sat gathered around the oil press, or during the grape harvest or religious feasts, she learned about and developed a deep sensitivity to their endless dramas.

Clandestinely she wrote and sent to a Rome newspaper her first story about the only life she knew: the primitive world of the Sardinian shepherds, peasants, and mountaineers. From the moment the story was accepted for publication, Cosima realized her vocation was to be a creative writer.

The second part of the novel develops the story of her achieving just that goal—albeit with considerable trembling and fear. Her deviation from the accepted role model of a Sardinian woman, her rebellion against her family's severe traditionalism, her aspirations, her projects, her first publishing contacts with magazines, her debut as a writer, and acclaim from her admirers on the "continent"—all are narrated with exuberance, vigor, and, by today's standards, considerable ingenuousness.

Her uninspiring love affairs, deglamorized even further by the villagers' aspersions, brought her into a love-hate relationship with the islanders and aroused in her a deep sense of dissatisfaction which served merely to reinforce the conviction of her own worth. Imposing on herself a strict personal and literary discipline, she sought, within the limits of her means, to give expression to the humble world of the people. After rigorously holding her imagination in check in her early books, she subsequently gave freer rein to her inner growth and maturation. The limpidity and transparency of Deledda's fully developed style convey equally convincingly a real landscape or a world of dreams. The flat grayness of her own restrictive life revealed in her early writings ultimately yielded to kaleidoscopic descriptions of the legends, myths, and fantasies[5] of an entire province of Italy. Cosima's *"bisogno/sogno"* was finally realized.

Perhaps Grazia Deledda may be compared with her contemporary, the American writer Willa Cather (1873-1947), who
also found her characteristic themes of spirit and courage in the
frontier region she had known in her youth (cf. *O Pioneers!*,
1913, and *My Antonía*, 1918).   In other novels, Cather, like
Deledda, relates the struggle of a talent to emerge from the con-
stricting life of the prairies and the stifling effects of small town
life.   Like Willa Cather, whose frequent visits to the American
southwest gave her an intimate acquaintance with a section of
the country destined to figure significantly in her works, Deledda
writes about the southwest part of *her* country, a piece of steep
land cut off from the continent by the sea, described in *Cosima* as
"a long, shiny sword lying at the foot of a cliff" (971).   *Cosima*,
however, is a book that goes far beyond the author's immediate
surroundings, beyond universal time into the mythical time of
magic rituals and creative writing.   It is a poetic array of narrative sources from which Grazia Deledda drew her original and
dramatic Sardinian novels, and at the same time told her own
story with deep perception and illumination.
   Ada Negri's (1870-1945)[6] slim volume, *Stella mattutina*,
tells poetically her own sad experience of social inferiority, likewise not in the first person singular but through the story of a
lonely and melancholy little girl, Dinin, whom she remembers
as part of herself: "I see—in time—a little girl" is the opening
sentence of the book.   Dinin is like Cosima: both have a burning
desire to observe, to know.   Even though the face of this little
girl seems far away and looks different from her own, it is Ada
Negri's countenance: a teacher without a vocation but determined to perform some kind of dignified work; a true poet and
short-story writer; and a militant socialist concerned about
workers' exploitation and the double enslavement of women, by
their employers and by their husbands.
   Dinin despises the humiliation suffered by her grandmother, first a cleaning woman and now a concierge (note that
this word derives from the Latin *conservus*, fellow slave); she
abhors the working conditions of her widowed mother, Vittoria,
a laborer in a wool-weaving factory in Lombardy.   Like the five
hundred other anonymous, tenacious women workers in the
factory, Vittoria lives a life of silence, submission, and solitude,
working thirteen hours a day, six days a week, and sometimes
even a half-day on Sunday—all for a mere pittance.   She pre-
tends, however, to be joyful, and sings her happy songs at home,
just to illude herself and Dinin.   Grandmother, mother, and

daughter all lodge together in a single, tiny room off the entrance of the wealthy tenants' manor-house, where the three
sleep in one large bed and together cook their daily fare of bread,
milk, and *polenta* (maize pudding). At night, when the older
women think Dinin is asleep, they read aloud serial romances
that open the child's mind to horizons beyond the little room,
and later, having discovered in a basement some dusty volumes
of Alexandre Dumas père and Emile Zola, she confesses they are
for her "like boarding a ship and crossing the sea" (21). The hallucinating intensity of Zola's cruel and corrupt world scars her
soul and bends her mind under the weight of humanity's tor-
ments and problems, but helps to convince her that in all her efforts—physical and mental—she must excel because she is poor.
Dinin is determined to become neither a subservient concierge
like her grandmother, nor an exploited factory worker like her
mother, nor a social derelict like her weak and ineffectual
brother, whose ambivalence she skillfully assesses: "He was tenacious only in his single great passion: books; and in his weak-
nesses: dancing, drinking, and loud, sterile discussions . . . [He
was] not sufficiently endowed with genial qualities to become an
artist: but not sufficiently dimwitted to stay between the tracks of
a humble job at 90 lire a month: not sufficiently a stray dog to
abandon himself completely to the night life of the underworld.
Ill at ease, everywhere. Unsatisfied, always. Without an enemy,
because too innocuous in his disarming vacuity: without a
friend, because the weak have no friends" (156-57). Dinin, on
the other hand, is all of a piece: feet planted firmly on the
ground, she stares in defiance at the pre-dawn morning star
(hence the title of the volume), rising very early to prepare to go
to the work that represents her chance for emancipation. Dinin,
like Sonia in Francesca Sanvitale's *Madre e figlia* (see Chapter
Six, below), will dedicate her efforts to her "family"—that is, her
mother. Stronger than Sonia, however, she vows to distinguish
herself in some way, some day, by taking up the cause of a larger
brotherhood of human beings. She is determined to lead a literary revolt on behalf of the proletariat and she knows that to render life a work of art she must use elements of the most humble
toil. Dinin lives in what she sees as a liquid flow of time, invisible, elusive, ungraspable, but measurable, at least, through her
own writings.

The youthful poverty of **Anna Maria Ortese** (see Chapter
Two, above) is described in her autobiographical novel *Poveri e
semplici* (Poor and simple, 1967), which won the Strega Prize for

that year.   The novel relates the period of her life spent as a struggling writer in post-World War II Milan, where she lived communally in penury with a group of young leftist intellectuals—poor, creative people full of idealistic dreams and hopes. Ortese's descriptive prose, in *Poveri e semplici*, comes close to sheer poetry. Her images of the city of Milan are pervaded with feelings of gratitude and love, quite different from the reactions she had earlier expressed towards the hostile, cold, concrete city in *Silenzio a Milano* (Silence in Milan, 1958), in which the spectral industrial city with its miserable underground system is represented, paradoxically, without noise, just as her miserable Naples was not washed by its bay. Once she achieves success as a writer, however, the heroine of *Poveri e semplici* finds peace and well-being. Her writing has wrought an alchemistic transformation of her poverty and her simplicity, which permits her to embrace with tenderness the two cities that symbolize Italy's farthest extremes.

Two novels with strongly autobiographical overtones are *Althénopis* (1981) and *Taccuino tedesco* (German notebook, 1987), by **Fabrizia Ramondino** (1936-   ), coeditor of an important anthology about her native city of Naples.[7]

Taccuino tedesco relates a metaphoric and initiatory trip by a young woman who feels herself excluded from, and unconnected to, "a universe of males and angels."[8]   Discovering in writing an effective escape from feelings of extraneousness and social laws that are repugnant to her, she returns to Germany, thirty years after her last youthful sojourn there, for the launching of the German translation of her first novel, *Althénopis*, whose heroine-narrator is, instead, a little girl with piercing black eyes.   The child portrays her submissive and suffering mother usually lying in bed with vinegar-soaked bands on her forehead to soothe her migraine or menstrual headaches, and, in the last part of the book, supine on her deathbed. In the end, the daughter proves stronger than her mother, whom she symbolically and heroically carries on her own slender shoulders.

The first two parts of the book are written in a mixture of literary-poetic and realistic-scatological styles, using a syntax closer to German or Latin than to Italian. In an interesting referential technique, Ramondino provides detailed footnotes—even though the work is a novel—that contain linguistic and learned explanations, sometimes rich in irony. The third part of the work—when this grown-up girl with piercing black eyes returns to Althénopis (Naples) from the North (Germany)—is written in a completely different style: staccato, telegraphic, and harsh. There is even an entire paragraph of sentences in the negative or containing the word cynicism or skepticism (242), as well as an entire chapter dwelling exactingly on the deterioration and decline of her senile mother. The third part is divided into short, terse chapters that sum up and are a commentary on the ills of the modern world, in which the reigning goddesses are no longer those of Althénopis, who charmed her in her childhood studies, but rather Anguish, Worry, Uncertainty, Insomnia—all bathed in neon light instead of her sorely missed Mediterranean sunshine (256).

Early in her career, Ramondino was to see parallels between her own life and that of Anna Maria Ortese, whom she chose as her literary model. She writes in *Taccuino tedesco*: "the beloved ghost was Anna Maria Ortese," and one critic has demonstrated that indeed Ramondino is the symbolic daughter of Ortese—the heir of the elder's creative patrimony. There is a strange link between the poetic universe of the older writer (ironic, visionary, disturbing, interwoven with an incurable existential sorrowfulness, and the impossibility of accepting the corruption of today's world) and Ramondino's forceful images, febrile anxiety, and passionality in describing her response to an incomprehensible world. The two also have in common the theme of exile and awareness of the fragility of new roots set down in new territories—real or metaphoric.[9]

I will hazard an even more generous comparison by likening the first two parts of *Althénopis* to Elsa Morante's *House of Liars* (see below). The female narrators of both novels try to change their lives, which are defined by outmoded traditions and conventions. In both works may be found keen, sensitive observations of a specific southern social milieu by two young girls who will find their own identities through the creative act of writing.

Fausta Cialente's (1900-   ) *Le quattro ragazze Wieselberger* (The four Wieselberger girls), which won the Strega Prize in 1976, is an outstanding historical-biographical-autobiographical novel embracing over sixty years of Italian history, from the period of *Italia irredenta* to the end of World War II.[10] The book describes the somewhat mythical and incongruous life style in "mitteleuropean" Trieste of four bourgeois sisters, one of whom is the mother of the narrator. Her father, a curious Italian antimilitarist military officer of Neapolitan origin, is the figure through whom the reader becomes privy to the fact that "Italians are rogues."

The narrator treats the fallacies of Triestine irredentism and of fascist anti-Semitism with strict ideological rigor, forcing the reader to retrace in his/her mind the positive elements in the history of the civil, tolerant city of Trieste over the past six centuries (39-42). By the outbreak of World War I, the Wieselberger family, inhabitants of a somewhat unreal Eden, was fast falling into decadence. The four sisters, victims of grandiose but illusory ideals, were being stalked by early twentieth-century evils lurking in the distance: corruption, cynical political interests, cruelties, masked lies, fanaticism, historical falsehoods, and coverups. To the racism that underlay the so-called Slovene question was added bourgeois indifference to the plight of workers, which inexorably led to mounting disorder and the rise of fascism in Italy. The analogy between the dissolution of a family and the parallel breakdown of a national society is clear. Cialente bears passionate yet persuasive witness to the individual and collective reasons for Italy's paroxysms during the first half of the twentieth century, and at the same time writes a telling tale of Italian bourgeois myopia during a process of deterioration[11]—even while sustaining the narrative tone of an autobiography.

During one of the many moves of the Wieselberger family to new residences in different cities to accommodate to the father's military career, the narrator joyfully discovers the empty attic of their apartment in Padua—a room of her own! Here she makes her first clandestine attempts at writing. A poor student because of the many changes in schools during her childhood, she nevertheless is a passionate reader and enjoys free verbal expression in writing. Putting down words on paper is her outlet, the satisfaction of a desire to formulate verbally her own ideas, and an expression of her own inner self. Discord between her parents and lack of friendships because of the family's frequent moves sadden her but leave her ample time for reflection and composition. Using correspondence with a musician cousin to polish her literary style, she becomes increasingly aware of the problems of writing as she throws away sheet after sheet of flat imitations of readings that had earlier impressed her: " . . . events often suggested themes to me, but before beginning to write I sheared from each fact everything that seemed to me to be useless, false or exaggerated, and what remained was so flat and impoverished that all I could decide was not to write anything, to leave intact the 'true' thing and the real feelings that it had aroused in me . . . " (141-42).

The narrator's never idle mother, an indefatigable worker continually engaged in writing letters, cooking and sewing, inspires her daughter's timorous admiration. As soon as her irresponsible husband leaves his military career to become a businessman in Milan, the mother knows she must act quickly: she obtains a voice-teaching diploma that permits her to earn the money her husband will proceed to squander. Thus, early in life, the daughter-narrator witnesses an example of a woman becoming independent through her work (like Dinin in *Stella mattutina*), even though this goes against the current of her bourgeois background and elicits cries of "scandal" from her husband's Neapolitan family. According to the ups and downs of her husband's business, the narrator's mother rents for voice lessons either a grand piano or an upright—one of the more amusing rise-and-fall leitmotivs in the novel.

That World War I was not a continuation of the romantic, pathetic Italian Risorgimento but rather a crass manoeuvre of an irritated and frightened bourgeoisie bent on stopping the advance of socialism was something the narrator and her family did not know at the time. The Triestine irredentists, possessed of a congenital scorn for workers, were lividly and myopically antisocialist; and the nation's bourgeoisie had unscrupulously thrown poor peasants and workers into a world conflict they did not understand but supported with meekness and resignation, as taught by the Church—"a church so sweet and mild for the rich and so severe for the poor" (172). After a long period of writing sterility, in the important year of 1917, the narrator finds new inspiration in the images of women protesting in the streets of Genoa, shouting for bread and peace. Women had taken the place of men as workers in the factories, and there was revolution in the air. The narrator-author realizes that finally women were in a position to look at reality, despite her father's protest that women belong "at home . . . and, even better, in the beds of their men" (181). The helpless but inventive narrator knows that "the only thing that remained for me to do . . . was to sit down and write, if only to forget the war and all our problems" (167).

The conclusion of the war in November, 1918, leaves the narrator disgusted, scornful, and filled with hatred for all forms of nationalism and racism. Feeling no patriotism whatsoever, she nevertheless bitterly joins the gleeful crowds in the streets but only because the useless massacre was over. Soon after the war, having married a Jew, she moves with her husband to Egypt to escape fascism in Italy. A note of interest for the contemporary reader is that the narrator finds the Middle Eastern countries to be open, free societies, so refreshing for Europeans of the time. Dazzled by the new culture she and her musician husband discover in Alexandria—French authors, contemporary composers, etc., as contrasted with fascist anticulture—hospitable reception is extended in their home, which becomes a base for antifascist activity abroad. Their cultural-artistic life lasted until the approach of World War II, when they were forced to flee from Egypt to Palestine. Only after the war, in 1946, is the narrator able to rejoin her mother in Italy, where she becomes a journalist and continues writing novels (see Chapter Seven, below).

Cialente's narrative style is, in fact, journalistic, although several highly literary descriptions and felicitous images may be found in the pages of *Le quattro ragazze Wieselberger*. Her sober presentation of events offers the reader good insights into the history and politics of Triestine irredentism and other matters of significant importance for Italy during the first half of the twentieth century. Although her viewpoint is critical and pessimistic, Cialente helps her readers flush out many deeprooted misconceptions, thus opening up possibilities for refining their thinking processes. Conscious of the need to salvage humankind from its lurid past by means of a moral, civil, social and political *engagement* with the future, Cialente goads her contemporaries a step closer to the noosphere by suggesting that they begin to shed their contradictions, cynicism, and hypocrisy of long standing.

Also recipient of the Strega Prize, in 1969, for an autobiographical novel *Le parole fra noi leggere* (Flighty words between us) is **Lalla Romano** (1909-   ), poet, novelist, short story writer, translator, art critic and painter. Prior to 1964, the characters in Romano's short stories and novels were fictional or at least partly invented (*Le metamòrfosi*, Metamorphoses, 1951; *Maria*, 1953; *Tetto Murato* [the name of a locality in Piedmont], 1957; and *L'uomo che parlava solo*, The man who talked to himself, 1961). The watershed year of 1964 marked Romano's entry onto the literary stage as the central character of her succeeding autobiographical novels—the genre that proved to be more suitable to her literary temperament. The first, *La penombra che abbiamo attraversato* (The twilight we have lived through, 1964), was inspired by the deeply traumatizing death of her mother. Returning to her birthplace, Ponte Stura, the author revisits the places she knew in childhood, renewing sentimental memories of her native village, its images and its episodes, which constitute for her an archetypal link with people and events of times past. According to one critic, more than a trip, her search to find the "secret" of that period of her life was like a pilgrimage to a sanctuary in the hope (or illusion) of obtaining some special favor, and this is what gives the work its quality of a voyage into time, a remembrance of things past, and an analysis of the most mysterious components of a magic childhood.[12]

Romano's on-the-spot search in nonlinear time is actually a search for the hidden reasons and the mythical meaning of a life engendered in the remote pre-World War I period. She tries to give each thing its place in history, its function in memory. The novel unfolds on two narrative planes, corresponding respectively to two different temporal planes: the present (in which the trip back to Ponte Stura, the contacts with persons and places revisited, and accompanying moods are described); and the past (in which memories surface, recollections unfold, places, persons, objects, situations, and landscapes are recalled in a process of free association).

The title of Romano's next book, *Le parole tra noi leggere*, is a line from the poetry of 1975 Nobel Prize winner, Eugenio Montale. Continuing in the *"letteratura della memoria"* vein, Romano still is engaged in an autobiographical search for things past; this novel, however, treats ironically and scornfully her difficult but tender relationship with her only son. Indulgence and solicitude, combined with resentment and aversion, are the hallmarks of the narration, which is realistic yet not completely devoid of fantasy. The mother's pathetically urgent need for affection, as well as her remorse, suffering, and regrets, are counterbalanced by her tenacious humorism, sharp irony, and objective self-criticism. Likewise, *L'ospite* (The guest, 1973), given a classical Freudian critical interpretation by Pier Paolo Pasolini, tells of a grandmother-grandson relationship in lyrical autobiographical tones, but also symbolizes the bittersweet intrusion of the unknown stranger whose presence upsets the order and the sense of the doting hostess' home.

Two subsequent works, *Una giovinezza inventata* (Youth invented, 1979) and *Nei mari estremi* (Faroff seas, 1987) form a sort of "diary-novel" of Romano's adult life. The first tells of her *éducation sentimentale* as a young bourgeoise in the 1920s at the University of Torino, where she lived in a women's dormitory managed by nuns—the same boarding institute frequented by Amalia Guglielminetti (see Chapter Six, below). *Nei mari estremi* is the story of her fifty years of married life to Innocenzo Monti; its title derives from a Hans Christian Andersen fable as well as from a painting in Romano's study depicting a ship sailing through the two walls of a split iceberg. The painting, for the author, represents a faroff place of deep silence, where the rarefied air is almost unbreathable. It is the place *"più in là"* — farther off—where her gentle husband dwelt for four months of devastating illness before his agonizing death. Like Andersen, Romano speaks with a soft, delicate voice, imagining cosmic life as pervaded with a breath of goodness.

The intimacy of the couple's married life, her husband's extreme humility and altruism, his repugnance of dirt and his ritual cleansing of himself are poignantly related in *Nei mari estremi*. The sensitive Innocenzo's first contact with death as a child had been painful: running through a field, he stepped on a chick, crushing out its life. Whenever he relates the story, he relives the horror of the episode and admits never having recovered from a sense of guilt and the mysterious remorse that accompanies unwilled evil (128).

Lalla Romano associates death not with horror, guilt, and remorse, but rather with absence: "Dying," she writes, "is setting out towards absence" (159), referring to a fading of the real into the pictorial world. She sees agony and the horror of death in terms of art—the cries, fury, and disfigurements evoked by Francis Bacon's demoniac "Triptych" (195). Just as the painting in her study came to represent the death struggle, her husband's figure, during the last month of his life, took on the features of Rembrandt's old men. There is artistry in Romano's description of his dying body under a dark green blanket, and in the end it is art that illuminates her on the significance of death: "In art it is essential to stop in time; in life, death does it for us" (210).

Regarding the intolerableness of physical pain, Romano writes: "part of my selfishness is the impossibility of seeing people suffer uselessly"; at the same time, however, she knows that sedatives cause a loss of memory and "life without memory is already death" (170). Her dilemmas are intensified by her impotence in the face of tragic illness and her desire for sleep as she sits reading and contemplating at the bedside of her husband slumbering under the effect of analgesics. When he awakens, she cedes to a moment of monstrous impatience in ministering to him while he, in his unbounded altruism, he who is dying, understands and takes pity on her. In a single sentence, Romano relates an entire parable (167).

Despite the lacunae and overall flatness of Romano's writings, the most recent of which are her collections of memories entitled *Un sogno del Nord* (Northern dream, 1989), and *Le lune di Hvar* (Moons of Hvar, 1991), they nevertheless have importance in any panorama of women's autobiographical works. Her highly introspective diary-novels are unfortunately marred by her "excessive autobiographism," which she herself recognized.[13] Her fanatic fidelity to the facts of her past existence and the minutiae of daily life limit the scope of her somewhat heavy, monotonous self-recounting novels. Unlike Cialente of *Le quattro ragazze Wieselberger*, and Ginzburg of *Family Sayings* (see below), who succeed in redimensioning their autobiographies into social sagas, Romano fails to reconstruct the history of her community; her novels, instead of conveying a collective forward movement, seem to mark time within the span of only one person's life.

* * *

Readers interested in knowing about the goings-on in the personal lives of Italy's cultural elite might skim *La fiorentina* (The Florentine, 1950), by writer, painter, and political figure **Flora Volpini**, remembered for her liaison with Guido Piovene. The elite residing in Rome at Via Lungara, 3, the thick-walled seventeenth-century building that stands between the Lincei National Academy and Regina Coeli prison, may be glimpsed in *La mia Kasbah* (My casbah, 1989) by **Fernanda Pivano**, translator, critic, and anthologist as well as novelist of some note.

Americans living in the United States during the McCarthy era and curious to know how they were perceived by an Italian woman writer might profit from a reading of *America postuma* (Posthumous America, 1972): in this diary-novel[14] **Silvana Giorgetti** relates her 1952-54 sojourn in the U.S.A. and confesses to "a certain resentment for its people, too rich, too efficient, too little tried by History" (9). The cover of her book—a piece of corrugated cardboard on which the title is splashed in red and black—bodes no good for America. Her postmortem analysis, taking the form of a regretfully short journal replete with tongue in cheek and perceptivity on subjects ranging from the slander tactics of Joseph McCarthy to the Cold War, from the

Progresso Italo-americano to her detainment at Ellis Island as a somewhat suspect leftist, is proffered with an underlying wit, good humor, and understandable bewilderment. Had the author expounded on her themes more fully and more deeply the reader would undoubtedly have been able to find richer reward in her self-recounting novel. *America postuma* is nonetheless valuable for its firsthand view by a member of the Italian intelligentsia of a segment of U.S. society involved in America's cultural and political development of the early 1950s. Giorgetti, with her advantage as a citizen of eternal Rome, exercises keen critical judgment and remarkable foresight in contemplating this late-born American—a country that creates such a state of mind in the author that her singular experience at the end of her sojourn reads like the script of a Buñuel film.

* * *

"I used to be absolutely horrified by autobiography. Horrified and terrified: because I was sorely tempted by the autobiographical genre . . . [but] I was absolutely terrified that I might be 'boring and sentimental' since I was aware of my strong tendency towards sentimentalism—a defect I found to be odious because it is feminine: and I wanted to write like a man," wrote **Natalia Ginzburg** in her preface to a short story entitled "La madre" (The mother, 1948).[15] After much solicitation, however, she yielded and wrote the autobiographical *Family Sayings*, considered her best work and awarded the Strega Prize in 1963. More than an autobiography and less than a chronicle, *Family Sayings* combines personal and historical elements, and the author, putting to profitable use her particular forms of irony, humor, and comicality, takes special care to avoid all forms of sentimentalism.

Natalia Ginzburg was born of a Jewish father and a Catholic mother, but neither of her parents practiced a religion. Her exceptional family was composed of the gruff father, an incorruptible scholar; the forever happily complaining mother; and the five poetically inclined children—the seven constituting a closely knit family unit whose irresistible vitality animates the pages of *Family Sayings*. Natalia, however, was anxious, quiet, and solitary in her childhood, victim of a spiritual solitude due in great part to her family's (and its cultural circle's) opposition to fascism, but also to the total absence of any religious sentiment, which excluded her from the world of believers without integrating her into any other world. For this reason, some of her early works display a desperate bitterness and inner malaise which have affinities with contemporary American narrative of the time, and which Ginzburg was beginning then to know and appreciate.

Mixing the private lives of the family with the events of Italian history and the climate of intellectual, antifascist Torino between the two world wars, *Family Sayings* becomes, in a sense, an antifascist chronicle seen through the eyes of a young girl, and in this Natalia Ginzburg succeeds where Lalla Romano fails. Ginzburg scrutinizes herself, but with outside happenings, persons encountered, and testimonial observations impinging on her consciousness; in Romano's works, the focus is on the self rather than on outward events.

Word portraits of some of the most famous political, social, literary, and academic figures are drawn by Ginzburg with the same sharpness and relief as her most obscure relatives and friends. Their home had become a refuge for escapees from fascism (such as the Socialist hero, Filippo Turati, and Adriano Olivetti, who was later to become a world-famous industrialist), as well as a meeting place for conspirators, including Natalia's future husband, Leone Ginzburg, confidant of her brother, Mario, who was to become one of Italy's famous political exiles.

The main passion of Leone Ginzburg, who had gone to Italy from Russia as a child, was politics, but he dedicated himself also to poetry, philology, and history. Sociable, knowledgeable, and possessed of an excellent memory, after his incarceration by the fascists as a dangerous conspirator he was pained to find the salons of Torino closed to him. Natalia, despite her father's protests that Leone did not have a "secure position," married him in 1938 during the period when Torino saw an influx of Jews fleeing from Germany. She skillfully conveys the growing sense of oppression in their circle as fascism appears to be lengthening its shadow, the racial campaign grows, and Jewish families leave or prepare to leave Italy. Leone, now a stateless person, is periodically arrested each time the King or a political authority sets foot in Torino.[16] (Leone Ginzburg later died in the German arm of Regina Coeli prison in Rome during the Nazi occupation; Natalia continued to use his name even after her second marriage to Gabriele Baldini in 1950).

One of the most pleasurable and perceptive parts of the book is the sensitivity the author brings to linguistic matters and lexical meanings (hence the world "lexicon" in the Italian title) in relation to the traits and qualities of her family members. The distinctive words and phrases used by her parents bind the family indissolubly and allow the five brothers and sisters, in later years, to relive their childhood and their former relationships: "one of those phrases or words would permit us to recognize each other . . . in the darkness of a cave, out of a million people. Those phrases are our Latin, the vocabulary of our past days, they are like the hieroglyphics of the ancient Egyptians or of the Assyro-Babylonians, they bear witness to a living nucleus that no longer exists but survives in its texts, saved from the fury of floods, the corrosion of time. Those phrases are the foundations of our family unity, which will survive as long as we are alive" (28).

Ginzburg's observations on the evolution of language and literature during and after World War II (171-73) are both discerning and illuminating. Right after the war, she writes, tongue in cheek, each one thought he was a poet and a politician. Whereas, during the war, reality had been seen as immobile and petrified behind a plate of glass, novelists and poets had fallen silent, and fascism had produced only arid, closed, sybilline dream-world poetry, after the war many new words and a general harvest of new ideas came into circulation. Reality seemed close at hand. In a long, impelling description of the "general harvest," which turned out to be sheer ephemerality, Ginzburg demonstrates that the shattering of the glass plate hiding reality was only an illusion. After an initial outburst of postwar enthusiasm, the language of poetry became confused with the language of politics, and writers fell back into their dream world, forgetting the brief interlude during which each individual really shared and participated in the life of the next person. The common basic error was the belief that everything could be transformed into poetry and words; this led to disgust with both, so that even true poetry and true words were silenced as writers became petrified in their boredom and existential nausea. "And the period that followed was like a hangover, a period of nausea, langor and tedium; and everyone felt . . . deceived and betrayed: both those who were living in reality, and those who possessed, or thought they possessed, the means for relating reality. And so each one set out once again, alone and discontent, on his own path" (173). Such penetrating analyses of the problems of Italy's literati, as well as of editorial suggestions regarding her own work, make *Family Sayings* a highly useful tool in gaining insight into the literary climate of postwar Italy.

Although Ginzburg's family lexicon—words flung across the dinner table, paternal reproaches, unconnected retorts, pet phrases, word games, and all the mysterious elements that characterize and bind the entity called "family"—is a language comprehensible only to those involved in the network of the author's recollections, the book nevertheless preserves its importance by confirming the author's sharp spirit of observation, her sensitivity, her cultural breadth, and her humorism. Ginzburg's *"letteratura della memoria"* not only is an evocative book of recollections, but also proffers a tacit resurrection, a new beginning, and a new entrée into present-day reality. Through her own life style as well as the message conveyed by the life style and the convictions of her family, Natalia Ginzburg, the lexicographer, is in step in helping to move humanity forward.

Other women writers who have recorded their personal recollections and revealed parts of their own lives in their published words are **Fleur Jaeggy**, in her Bagutta Prize-winning *I beati anni del castigo* (1990), which describes the voluptuousness of obedience and the blessedness of punishment in a poetically evoked boarding school; **Susanna Agnelli** (see Chapter Seven, below) in *Vestivamo alla marinara* (We always wore sailor suits, 1975) and *Addio, addio mio ultimo amore* (Farewell, farewell my last love, 1985); and **Anna Banti** (see Chapter three, above) in *Un grido lacerante* (A piercing cry, 1981), in which a woman married to a university professor feels such deep affection and admiration for her husband that her esteem for him provokes a disturbing awareness of her own insignificance. Recognizing her limits in her own vocation as a writer, Banti describes her personal sense of dissatisfaction and futility, unmitigated by various attempts on her part to perform regular remunerative work and to lead a complete social life. Similarly, the novels of **Marise Ferro** (1906-1991), a central figure in Milan's literary coterie until her recent death, reveal the shadow cast on her own intellectual exuberance by her two illustrious husbands, Guido Piovene and Carlo Bo, as well as the general difficulties faced by women seeking their place in society (*Disordine* [Disorder, 1932]; *La ragazza in giardino* [The girl in the garden, 1976]; *La sconosciuta* [The unknown woman, 1978]).

The microcosm of a girls' boarding school in Rome is the community in which **Alba de Céspedes** (see Chapter Six, below) develops an embryo adolescent into complete maturity, in a one-way process evoked by the title of the book: *Nessuno torna indietro* (There's no turning back, 1938). Although the work was banned by the fascists in 1940, it was nevertheless highly acclaimed in Italy and abroad, and has been translated into no less than twenty-four languages. Focusing particularly on one of the novel's eight young women whose lives, characters, and decisions are depicted, the novel explores in depth the heroine's guilt on the one hand, and, on the other, her longing to forget the past and begin life afresh. The double thrust of the work lies in its manifest inducement to defy preestablished social schemes but the inevitable necessity as well of expiating the "sin" committed against institutions and traditions.

"The real novel, for me, consists in the connecting of points of the plot with episodes of my own life,"[17] wrote **Gianna Manzini** (1896-1974); accordingly, she kept a diary from which she freely drew material for the plots of her novels.

Manzini began her long literary career in 1926, among a sparkling group of Florentine writers and poets—the intellectual elitist group known as "Solaria" that helped to mold her into a refined stylist. The extreme delicacy and dreaminess of her poetics tended, however, to become less ethereal in her later works, in which she continued to search for the poetical identity of her characters but adopted a more vivid, unfeigned, and psychologically comprehensible style. Opposed to the externalizations of the neorealistic novel, she staunchly defended the idea that writing is helping oneself and others to understand, and that social understanding must be filtered through the personal—and not vice versa. Identifying often with the male character in her books, Manzini, even though greatly concerned about women's rights, claimed that such an identification helped to make her more "honest." Many of the characters may in fact be considered her *alter ego*, for her works center on the topics uppermost in her mind: the effects on character of a secluded childhood; chronic illness; early death; existential anguish; and the artistic mission. She treats these themes many times over in a series of works written from the later 1940s onward, which may be seen in essence as a single autobiographical novel. Her personal experiences and human contacts are at the heart of each work and her "honesty" bids her to bring to each of her poetic, musical portraits a certain delicate realism as well as highly accurate representation.

Manzini describes her own emotions and inner stimuli, especially vis-à-vis her mother—a woman of bourgeois extraction and renunciatory character, and her father—a forceful man of anarchical sentiment who, though he tenderly loved his fam-

ily, left if for a life of rebellion, privation, imprisonment, and
early death (see below).

With moving sensitivity, Manzini attempts to discover
the spiritual and material origins of the deep loneliness that
pervades both herself and her characters. All seem to be living a
winter of discontent. Basic to Manzini's self-recounting works is
the theme of an existential loneliness that stems from her difficult relationship not with society, but with herself. Anguish and
self-displeasure emerge inexorably from her subtle and sensitive
characterizations.

The short step from solitude to death leads consonantly to
another recurring theme in Manzini's works: solitude as pre-
lude to a death that exalts the immortal soul and degrades the
enfeebled body. Demonstrating particular skill in evoking physical sensations with their correlated psychological effects,
Manzini studies the relationship between the spirit and what
she calls the "dear prison" of the body, each a separate unity,
locked in a macabre dance. The body, wracked with the pain of
its deteriorating organs, must surely decline, but the creative
spirit (writing, art) constitutes sufficient reason for living, and
gives the body the necessary support to defeat its afflictions.
Thus, Manzini is able to come to terms with her own bodily ill-
nesses as the tangible expression of a life of the spirit, and, in a
reciprocal exchange, her spiritual emotions are incorporated into
her physical essence. In one of her short stories, Manzini had
written: "a woman is really a woman when she is ill,"[18] implying that sickness can sharpen and exalt sentimental qualities
characteristic of women. An important message for her readers,
then, is that pathetic attitudes are not in keeping with greatness,
and that illness can sometimes bring inner happiness, enrich the
life of the spirit, and provide moments of extreme lucidity regarding human existence.

Death, for Manzini, is neither the final moment of existence nor the interruption of life's flow, but rather a necessary
moment of existence itself, infinitely prolonged in the memory
of others. Both conqueror (when it upsets one's destiny) and
conquered (when vanquished by art), death forever stalks
Gianna Manzini like a "bird of prey," especially in the last years
of her life when she had become sick and frail. Fearful that the
lurking enemy might preclude completion of *Ritratto in piedi*
(Standing portrait, see below), when she finally saw its publication she expressed satisfaction at having won over death. Like
the Nietzsche of the eternal recurrence, Manzini believes that,

through art, the impress of eternity may be stamped upon our lives.

Sickness has generally been identified as the real protagonist of *La sparviera* (The sparrow hawk, Viareggio Prize, 1956), the most famous and symbolic of Manzini's novels, and autobiographical even though the protagonist is a man. The sparrow hawk, a bird of prey, is a metonymy for the persistent bronchial cough that plagues the central figure, Giovanni Sermoni. The carnivorous bird that insinuated itself into Giovanni's life in his early childhood serves to give his short existence the additional dimension of domination by an irrational force. His life, he complains, has been spent on the leash of a sparrow hawk that leads or restrains according to its will. From kindergarten games to adolescence, the time of his pure and luminous friendship with a bright young girl named Stella, the cough had stalked, waiting to seize and devour him during his happy moments. As a university student and aspiring actor, at tryouts for the role of Hamlet opposite Stella filling the role of Gertrude, the parts of the doomed Queen and Prince are a presage of their own untimely death. Because of the sparrow hawk, Giovanni is forced to renounce his theatrical ambitions; and the intense, ecstatic, ungraspable love that grows between him and Stella will end with her tragic death. Giovanni, prey of the tyrannical force that won the struggle between his body and his spirit, also dies after lifetime persecution by an occult presence. Yet the tyrant is precisely that force that gives Giovanni's personality its exceptive dimension. It places him in a different, personal world, where his imagination and his memories are given free rein. Sickness and death collaborate in heightening Giovanni's awareness of the relationship between his "dear prison" and his spirit, its house guest.

A striking musical parallel to the literary concept of *La sparviera* may be found in Richard Strauss's tone poem, "Death and Transfiguration" (1889), an equally lyrical representation of the individual's struggle against death: a motionless sick body lying under heavy blankets is oppressed by indescribable suffering (accompanied by a simple melodic motif). To this first theme is added a more complex one, corresponding to the realization that the sick body belongs to a man. The living man thinks back over the events of his past life throughout the third theme entitled "childhood souvenirs." The fourth theme corresponds to "death's first attack," while the fifth is a perfectly simple descending chromatic scale representing the man's desperate attempt to subjugate death. A short-lived victory is possible only through recourse to "lessons of thought" (the sixth theme) and the archetypal belief in immortality. Distant memories return, this time arising from adolescence, and the corresponding theme is made up of melodic elements of the earlier motifs. After a brief episode dedicated to the "man in love," represented by an ascending chromatic scale, some fragmented elements of the earlier themes are heard again, after which the episode of the struggle against death is repeated with greater impetus, interlaced with the theme of Transfiguration that transforms the sacrifice of a human life into authentic art.

Manzini's Campiello Prize-winning novel, *Ritratto in piedi* (1971), is dedicated in subject and sentiment to her father, the anarchist Giuseppe Manzini, staunch defender of justice, but repudiated by her mother's bourgeois family. The author shows deep remorse for having neglected her father during the years of his exile while she was scintillating in Florence, and also for the long delay in paying homage to him after he died of a heart attack following an ambush by a group of fascists near Pistoia. Even more than a personal recollection, *Ritratto in piedi* is a sort of "parahuman" dialogue with her dead father, who communicates to her a message of goodness and love. Likewise, *Sulla soglia* (On the threshold, 1973), a magisterial work written before her death a year later, is an affectionate remembrance of her mother's tenderness and care. As death's shadow looms above her, Manzini looks it square in the face as an enemy to be routed. She finds her memories give her the necessary strength to accompany her deceased mother on an imaginary and symbolic voyage.

Thus, well ahead of contemporary psychiatrists who now claim that illness and pain can help one to live a fuller inner life,[19] Gianna Manzini plunged into her deepest self to study the links between mind and body. She knew that illness snatches off masks and reveals the most hidden aspects of the patient. Whereas writing, for her, had first been an escape from the real world of suffering, it became her way of beating illness and death, and cultivating hurt for the sake of art and eternity.

Elements of **Marina Jarre**'s eclectic life—her birth in Riga, Lettonia, of a Russian Jewish father and an Italian Waldensian mother, her involvement as a partisan in the resistance, etc.— color her writings, the latest of which, *Ascanio e Margherita*, was among those being considered for the Strega Prize in 1990. *I padri lontani* (Faraway fathers, 1987) is an autobiographical

novel relating her solitary childhood, her father's mistreatment
of her mother, and the disillusionment of her own marriage.
Her husband—"he the artist, I the ant,"—is a copy of her evasive
and unapproachable father. It is not, however, against men that
Jarre protests. Her hurt and anger are aimed against those
women in her life who denied her their affection and raised her
as though she were a rival.[20]

Elsa Morante's self-recounting novels are in a category of
their own. Poignant, imaginative, complex, confounding, and
ambiguous—all these adjectives are applicable to *House of Liars*
(begun in 1943 and published in 1948), and its mirror-volume,
Aracoeli (1982, her last novel, written between 1976-81 and published a year before her suicide attempt in 1983).

Most critics agree that the voice of the fabulist-protagonist-
narrator (Elisa) who lives in the arcane house of liars is Elsa
Morante's own. In *Aracoeli*, the sex, the quest, and the illusions
of the narrator are inverted, but the sensitive reader cannot fail
to perceive Morante's own presence in the solitary figure of
Emanuele, the boy who begged his barber to make his beard stop
growing. Both Elisa and Emanuele have Morante's own obses-
sion with the dead, and both novels reveal the author's death
wish. (The narcissistic desire for death—a theme that has found
its place in Italian feminist literature since the late 1970s—is expressed in two works by **Ginevra Bompiani**: *Le specie del sonno*
[Kinds of sleep, 1975] and an ironical novel, *Mondanità*
[Worldliness, 1980]).

Both the "southern" and the "northern" components of
Morante's inspiration interact in her self-recounting novels.
The southern ingredients are constituted by myths, rhapsody,
nostalgia, crudeness of taste, and fondness for gorgeous display,
while the northern elements include a fascination with fables,
legends, mysteries and spirits. Combining the two, Morante
concocts her intricate tales in a highly romantic literary style.

Aracoeli (the name of Emanuele's Andalusian mother is
Aracoeli Muñoz Muñoz) is a reconstruction of fragmentary
events in the narrator's life, reflected in the mirror and the
memory of his parents. The zigzagging course of the narration
takes the reader to a small town in southern Spain, El Almendral, which Elsa Morante had imagined and fully described even
before she knew it actually existed.[21]

Setting out in search of his mother whose past had always
been kept a secret, Emanuele undertakes a double journey: the
physical trip to the Andalusian village where she was born, near

Almerìa (meaning "mirror" in Arabic), and a mental trip, winding through his childhood and adolescence. He relives his early attempt to take his dead sister's place in order to gain his mother's love, and his later fall into loneliness, torment, and dissipation. He relates his life and his symbolic dreams in which he often assumes the shape of a rat. Using cinematographic techniques, Morante flashes before the reader's eyes rapid sequences: Emanuele's envy of the virility of his father, a naval officer whom he idolized in his absence; his adolescent cultivation of a double who has all the qualities he lacks; his sexual aberrations, drug addiction, and his persistent suicidal tendencies. This series of pictures produces the blurring effect of a damaged film, but the poetic language, the magic images, the landscape descriptions, plus occasional touches of real humor add more dimensions to Morante's versatility.

Thirty-six years after his mother's burial in Rome's Verano cemetery,[22] the forty-three-year-old Emanuele, lonely, unloved, and unlovable, bored with his job in a Milan publishing house, begins his search for the dead Aracoeli, setting out into nonlinear time and primordial space with *enthusiasmòs* (divine invasion)—a godling more "like an animal, sniffing for the odors of its own den" (9). The restlessness and earthiness of Emanuele (similar to Morante's) are frequently evoked: "I am an animal," "I don't know what kind of animal I am," etc. But before the disoriented animal can reach its destination— Almerìa—the place of his love tryst with his mother, his life story must unfold and the reappearing image of Aracoeli Muñoz Muñoz must be clearly fixed—framed in the mirror of his mind. The indelible portrait of Aracoeli is a semihuman mother holding her child in her arms carrying him off to her lair.

The mystery of the mother-child relationship had always been kept hidden from him. Was he born out of wedlock? Did she die leaving him an orphan? The two interchanging forms of Aracoeli, both of which he loves, stir his "*rimembranza apocrifa*" (apocryphal remembrance): one mother buried in the Verano cemetery and the other, an Andalusian girl forbidden to marry the man she loved. Only after long years of common-law cohabitation were Emanuele's parents finally permitted to marry and live together in a fashionable section of Rome, where the child no longer was kept in hiding. The trauma of the secrecy of his early existence accounts for Emanuele's love-hate relationship with his mother: he sometimes sees her as a beautiful creature, sometimes a deformed, cruel mother who casts off her infant once she becomes tired of playing with her "toy" (103). Towards the end of her life, the mentally ill Aracoeli becomes oversexed, obese, and insomniac and she is finally driven to abject prostitution. He tears from his neck the death-repelling magic amulet his superstitious mother gave him and hurls it away.

After Aracoeli's death, her horribly deformed body returns to take vengeance on her son, taunting him incessantly until he finally is able to stop dreaming of her. As he travels now to her native village, incidents which had been forgotten return to memory like hallucinations. Flashbacks, trick photography, optical illusions are played out in words (as, e.g., Emanuele's myopia, which permits him either to see the world in all its ugliness, with hard, brutal marks on human faces, reminiscent of the faces that shock the myopic girl in Anna Maria Ortese's *Il mare non bagna Napoli*, or, by removing his eyeglasses, allows him to reduce humankind to formless larvae and fuse objects on a screen for a shadow play).

Emanuele's trip culminates at El Almendral: a few houses, a bastard dog, and everyone in the village bearing the name Muñoz Muñoz! Returning to Rome, he seeks out his father, now a poverty-stricken old drunkard who still loves Aracoeli and has moved to the slum neighborhood near the Verano cemetery to be close to her. Emanuele bursts into tears of love for the decrepit old officer. Yet when the father dies, Emanuele does not weep because, like Elsa Morante, he belongs to that category of "certain individuals more inclined to weep out of love than over death" (328).

The feminine counterpart of Emanuele is Elisa in *House of Liars*, a bewitching tale that lends itself to innumerable interpretations. A solitary girl, little loved by her father, and less by her mother, Elisa is what would today be called the "growing-up-grotesque" archetype: an "old child," an "ill grown youth" with the eyes of a "wild boy," timid, awkward, with a tendency to love too intensely, and a propensity to overdramatize chance meetings and casual phrases. Such epithets do not belie Elsa Morante's own traits, nor is it difficult to discern other autobiographical data hidden in the pages of the book. *House of Liars* seems, in fact, to be an autobiography in the first person singular, transformed into a long dream epic.

Elisa, whose pabulum consists of fables, fairy tales, and sacred legends, relates, as though they were her own memoirs, a

romantic and fanciful love story of her mother, Anna, of humble origin, and a first cousin, Eduardo, a Sicilian nobleman.

Told in fable-like terms of bewitchment (cf. the book's Italian title, *Menzogna e sortilegio*, falsehood and sorcery), Anna's
love-at-first-sight of the fabulous Cousin sitting regally in a
horsedrawn carriage is a tale in which the story-book couple, far
from marrying and living happily ever after, is doomed to play
out an inexorable tragedy. Anna will become the wife of the
unloved, pockmarked Francesco de Salvi (Elisa's father), Eduardo will die prematurely of tuberculosis, and both families
will plunge into insanity and calamitous deaths. Young Elisa's
mind is plagued by the same confusion that afflicts the minds of
the adults surrounding her; her imagination, wild and sick like
theirs, is caught up in their game of lies. Becoming completely
disoriented during her mother's final agony, she loses her very
sense of time and place—almost a preview of Morante's own
hydrocephalus (excess of fluid in the cranium, resulting in mental deterioration), to which she refers in the novel as "that fan-
tastic illness that was later to assail me" (501).

Young Elisa reconstructs in minute detail the story of her
parents and grandparents, partly on the evidence of memories
and tradition, partly through her own imaginative efforts. The
history that emerges has the quality of a "dreamy arabesque."[23]
She tries to penetrate its meaning, spending her nights recalling
past events that seem to become episodes of her own life. In the
process of putting into order the material for narration, a natural
movement between reality and fancy comes into play, and fine
analyses of her own sentiments during real as well as imaginary
events make for even greater confusion. Yet, the reader is forced
to believe that everything is true. At the same time, she herself
admits that her writing is a product of magic and fantasy; she repeatedly uses the descriptive adjective *larval* in its original sense
of specter or mask, now convincing the reader that all is false.
Elisa states clearly that her family tree is infested with lies and
that her parents "know no happiness outside of falsehood" (21).
Through the lie, she combines memories of herself and of her
family, and through the metaphor of the theater, place *par excel-
lence* for the lie, she finds a substitute for life as well as a stage
for her characters' drama. Commonplace objects take on
"fabulous elegance" and "miraculous luxury" (420); the worthless objects revered by her parents impress her as a child
although in reality she knows that they are "execrable adorn-
ments." In a sober and controlled style, she chronicles the char-

acters' lives *paralleled by the lives of the figments of their imag-ination*. This superimposition, combined with what she calls the "wine and opium" effect of her own imagination, provide the key to the reading of *House of Liars*. Elisa involves the reader in the construction of both her primary and secondary characters, all of whom take on a kind of eternalized existence through the technique of capitalizing the first letter of Reader, Cousin, Our Lady, Death, Knight, Matador, etc. Each chapter of *House of Liars* appropriately bears a title that is the crux of a short story or tale of wonder tinged with magic medievalism ("Saints, Sultans and Grand Captains in my bedroom," "Francesco's brief sojourn in purgatory," "Brief and negligible apparition of a false nun," etc.). In her dialogue with the reader, she speaks confidentially, or playfully holds developments in suspense. At the same time she often goes off at a tangent only to call herself to order—"to go back to what I was saying"—in story-teller fashion. She evokes and takes leave of her minor characters as though she were an orchestra conductor, involved yet detached from the marriages, liaisons, intrigues, and catas-trophes of the players.

Thus, the novel must be read as the blossoming of an illu-sion. Characters are out in search of their mythical Mothers, Fa-thers, Prince Charmings, and heroes in any guise to whom they can offer blind devotion. They wander through magic looking glasses and are tricked by religious sham. Elisa finds her charac-ters in her imagination, during that "melancholy hour between light and dark" (308).

Full daylight, however, brings a perception of crushing re-alities: dashed hopes for honor, title, and wealth, unrequited love, and unslaked thirst for friendship. Only the earthy figure of Rosaria, woman of loose morals, illiterate prostitute, "mala femmina," as the southerners call her, turns out to be genuine, charitable, affectionate, sincere. It is she who takes pity on the orphaned Elisa, who had been raised like some strange, domesti-cated animal, bringing her into her home and offering her a semblance of maternal protection and love. (It is of interest to note that the female characters in *House of Liars*—A n n a , Rosaria, Eduardo's mother Concetta, who prays proudly and dramatically in church and performs other histrionic ceremoni-als for her son's recovery from his illness, are entirely *whole*, while the male characters—Eduardo, Elisa's father Francesco de Salvi, etc. are fickle, vacuous, voluble, ungrateful, confused be-ings with split personality structures.)

Up to the very end, Elisa had persisted in seeing as a beautiful, splendid, oriental madonna the mother who was incapable of expressing love for her daughter. Feeling alone even when her daughter is present in her room, Anna is the one who develops in Elisa the need for creating imaginary companions for a world of dreams. Anna is the one whose strange influence drives Elisa to seek the company of the shades of the defunct—evanescent appearances that gradually take possession of the girl's mind and wield the upper hand in her life. Finally, however, as Anna lies on her deathbed, victim of mental deterioration, Elisa drops into reality, losing the illusion of her mother's beauty. Anna's death causes the collapse of the house of liars and the end of Elisa's very existence, for her magic-mirror trick show is now over. The descriptive and psychological fiction is overturned as Elisa, who had populated her daily life with phantasmata, masks, and caracoling words finally faces squarely the realities of insanity and death.

The disenchanted Elisa now has only one last hope of showing pity for the dead figures in her past life: by narrating the story of their lives and searching for their destinies. She heeds their voices, which free her from the loneliness of her room. The formula for freeing herself from the magic spell is to invoke their names in her heart, thereby gaining their release and her own deliverance as well.

The small, unnamed, backward town in "il mio triste mezzogiorno" (my sad South)[24] of Elisa's chronicle is accurately described by Morante in its customs, traditions, and superstitions. The restricted mentality of the ignorant townspeople, and their hypnosis by church hocus pocus, lend their support to Elisa's games of fantasy. Descriptions of the town are extraordinarily vivid—as though Morante herself had lived there. Her oscillations between fable-like amplification and exact historic connotation permit the town to become inhabited by a petty bourgeois social class so disillusioned that, by lying to itself and using the instrument of unreality, it reaches the point of fascism.[25] Morante's imaginative tale serves both truthfulness and history and, in fact, the reader cannot fail to sense that *House of Liars* was written during the darkest war years, even though the war and fascism are not mentioned in the book. In the dusty streets, in the dark human figures, in the blind cruelty of individuals towards each other, fascism is undeniably present.

Perhaps the oppressive atmosphere of the 1940s and the modern existential condition is what Morante intended to sym-

bolize by the "Cavalieri della Trista Figura" (Knights of the Woe-
ful Countenance), who appear in Chapter 3 of the novel and rear
their grieving heads throughout the work. Devoid of all moral
grandeur, they can offer Elisa no vision of a better world. Her
only possibility, then, is to abandon herself totally to her readings[26] and fantasies, accepting the creative power of the lie and
the relieving effects of the hoax. Only after the death of her
adoptive mother, Rosaria, when she is left alone with her memories, will Elisa be able to discern the importance of her bound-
less fantasies: "I see all the symbols and signs [of the drama of my
youth] printed in my mind, and many of the ones that seemed
absurd or arcane to me then, today have been translated by my
experience into their real significance" (434).

The fable-like and at the same time cruel, bitter atmosphere of *House of Liars* lends the book its power and uniqueness. Morante's history is composed of the sum of all the little
stories of common people, and when any sympathy is expressed,
it is invariably for those who do not succeed in integrating
themselves in a system of dominant values and have a substantially anarchic concept of society. (In this respect her preferences
are similar to those of Gianna Manzini.)

Morante exploits the widest range of writing techniques,
muddling reality and illusion and displacing geographically defined places. She is a completely new novelist, using old instruments and old narrative techniques, but everything in her
work is original. Natalia Ginzburg has said that the miracle of
great books is to make the reader feel what is lurking behind
his/her shoulders without ever naming it.[27] In this respect,
House of Liars is the miracle of a great book.

Chapter Five

The Epistolary Novel

Umberto Eco is quite right when he points out that the reader of a novel written as a series of letters must feel involved, and that the circumstances surrounding the character must have contemporary associations.[1] The epistolary, by its very nature, is an exchange implying reciprocity, and a colloquy mediated by writing, as well as a sublimation of the need to communicate without expectation of a reply. It further represents an impelling need to extend oneself, and often is motivated uniquely for the pleasure of baring one's soul. This is why women have generally excelled as letter writers, but their distinction in the genre must also be ascribed to their greater reflectivity and introspection. In addition, being more confined to the home, women have more time to face the "uncertain process of letter writing" referred to by George Eliot in her *Life and Letters*.

That the epistolary novel is a facile form is belied by Virginia Woolf's reflection that a letter, unlike a private confession, is a precise literary mechanism in which style and affective ties are balanced. The author of the epistolary novel must allow the personages to create themselves from within and the reader to experience their vicissitudes through his/her own mind as the events occur instead of being informed of them by an all-knowing narrator. The writing of a novel in letter form is fraught with difficulties and the genre can easily become clumsy. The author must know how to set up the characters in harmony or in conflict with each other, then ostensibly remove him/herself in order to dictate the correspondence from behind the scenes, plumbing minutely and critically the thoughts that the characters reveal.

Several famous letter-writers are included in this volume for their novels. **Sibilla Aleramo**'s *Quel viaggio chiamato amore* (That journey called love) is a series of love letters tinted with the sadness and futility of life to her injurious poet friend, Dino Campana. *Lettere a Elio* (Letters to Elio), a later correspondence, written in her eighties, is filled with maternal affection and protective solicitude for the budding poet, Elio Fiori. **Annie Vivanti** is well known for her letters to an outstanding nineteenth-century literary figure, Giosuè Carducci. **Maria Messina** kept up a devoted correspondence with her fellow Sicilian, Italy's most important verist writer, Giovanni Verga. **Amalia Guglielminetti** wrote *Lettere d'amore* (Love letters to Guido Gozzano); and several of **Matilde Serao**'s short stories are written in the form of epistolary exchanges. In addition, three chapters of **Neera**'s *Una passione* (see Chapter Six, below) also contain letters that constitute the crux of the nascent love between the hero and heroine (who had not yet met) and offer interesting commentaries on signets, seals, and calligraphy.[2] In **Elsa Morante**'s *House of Liars* (see Chapter Four, above), untextualized letters play an important part throughout the novel, the submerged story being a narrative in epistolary form, which mother Anna writes in the secluded bedroom of her silent apartment.[3] The letters written by women protagonists in three of Gina Lagorio's novels (see Chapter Six, below) serve both as a structuring device as well as a form of liberation from restlessness or a confession of unhappiness.[4] **Gabriella Guidi Gambino**'s novel, *Ti scrivo per confessarti* (I'm writing to confess, 1989) hinges on a series of letters written between 1905-1914.

The earliest original Italian literary prose consisted, in fact, of letters, which followed certain medieval rhetorical rules. Prescribed standards included use of the *cursus* (i.e. rhythmical patterns for the endings of clauses and sentences), rhymes or assonances, and abundant figures of speech and play on words. Samples of this rhetorical prose style are generously sprinkled throughout **Maria Bellonci**'s historical novels (see Chapter Three, above) and their authenticity is guaranteed by her sources: manuscripts found in Vatican archives and State national libraries. Although not strictly speaking an epistolary novel, the seven chapters of one of Bellonci's historical novels, *Rinascimento privato*, contain twelve unanswered letters dated 1501-1533 and ten chapter sections entitled "Stanza degli orologi" (Room of the Clocks), which together weave three decades of sixteenth-century history experienced from inside the walls of

the Gonzaga palace in Mantua. The Renaissance historical matter contained in the novel are the events surrounding the rise
and fall of Ludovico Sforza of Milan, the splendor of Rome's
papal courts from Julius II to Leo X, the defeat of the lofty re-
public of Venice, the invasions of Italy under the French kings
Louis XII and Francis I, and the terrifying sack of Rome in 1527.
The twelve letters to Isabella d'Este, wife of Francesco II Gonzaga
of Mantua, are from an invented character, an English priest of
the Roman Curia, Robert de la Pole,[5] while the ten "Room of the
Clocks" sections function like a freely swinging pendulum regu-
lating the movement of the book, as Isabella ponders vicissitudes to the music in counterpoint of the costly, artistic clocks.
Her delicate personifications of her hundred clocks, and her
preference for the clock that is six hours slow (giving her additional time for reflection) are memorably drawn by Maria Bellonci, who herself seems to be ineluctably caught up in the contradictory clocks' search for a universal truce in the discordant
measurement of time (235).

Even though Isabella d'Este relates her story in the first
person singular, it is rather through the letters of Robert de la
Pole that an objective "I/eye" captures the character and portrait
of this exceptional and ideal woman. Having liberated herself
from society's restrictions, Isabella threw herself into a quest for
knowledge, mastering astrology, horoscopy, and herbal cures (so
necessary for her husband's syphilis symptoms and her own resulting gonorrhea). She became the supreme teacher for her son
who was later to assume power; she never failed in her marital
fidelity and responsibility, but still was able to impose her demands for individual rights. Isabella imagines the lives of her
male counterparts as arid and unadorned—"intent only on the
physicality of eating, sleeping, drinking, arms-drilling, always
struggling with things material"—whereas the intuitive world
of women is "illuminated with benign apparitions" that could
so much improve the male world (224). Her husband had once
confided to her how manly he felt when he heard the jingling
sound of an artistically designed medal or jewel hanging from a
necklace hitting against his breastplate. "And if it weren't so,"
Isabella observes astutely "why would kings and princes and
even the pope load themselves down with gold and gems?
These symbols of [the male] condition will never cease being active" (288).

De la Pole characterizes Isabella as "a feminine intellect
independent in itself yet accepting all attachments with earthly

life" (544), and "one of those very rare creatures who live their freedom, invented day by day, according to the light and dark of their own truths" (545). It was under her impetus that humanists and artists congregated in Mantua, transforming the city and bringing the Mantuan lordship to the height of its prestige. Palaces and villas were lavishly commissioned and splendidly adorned; the finest artists and writers found employment there: Baldassare Castiglione, Boiardo and Ariosto, Berni and Bembo, Andrea Mantegna and Perugino, Raphael, Giulio Romano, Leonardo, Titian, Monteverdi, and many others—all of whom move about in the pages of Bellonci's novel, as Isabella follows the genesis of their works.

As soon as her husband is taken prisoner by the Venetians, Isabella, braving the power of Emperor Maximilan and Louis XII, King of France, steps into the role of ruler and gradually becomes Mantua's governing force. She wastes no time with court frivolities: lopping off in a dramatic gesture the golden braid of one of her silly ladies-in-waiting, she brandishes it defiantly.

She is capricious, fiery, demanding, irritated when her pregnancies prevent her from riding on horseback, disappointed when she bears girls because she knows that her society demands of these daughters their total submission. Unless they succeed in becoming powerful political figures like herself, Isabella di Chiaromonte, and Lucrezia Borgia, women are doomed to obliteration in Italy's male-dominated society.

In a brief colloquium with Nicolò Machiavelli, Isabella's convictions are vindicated. The political philosopher tells her: "To command strongly, my lady, one must be strong. And you are strong. Humaneness finds its place only in private life. Whoever is not high-spirited cannot command a State" (175). Isabella succeeds in obtaining her husband's liberation from captivity, defying "half the world, emperor, king of France, Venice, Pope, and without failing to carry out a single requirement of the chancellery and of the office of podestà" (178). Discernment, indulgence, and double entendre mark Isabella's observations of the goings-on in Rome: " . . . nothing is comparable to the Roman court where in a lofty hall young cardinals in their sumptuous purple, in figured steps dance to cadenced music with ladies and damsels dressed in beautifully worked striped embossed brocade and satin . . . Dresses and capes ripple in slow motion with an almost sacred majesty . . . and if they should become the slightest bit ruffled, they are rigorously held in check by rhythmic constraint" (269). At the same time, however, Isabella knows that history is cyclical: negotiations between Pope Leo X and King Francis I of France, ostensibly for a "universal peace," mask sly manoeuvering for power, dominion and territory, because " . . . heads of state prefer division to union in order to achieve a stable peace" (276).

In homage to Isabella's wisdom and achievements, Robert de la Pole, signing himself her "slave" and declaring himself ready to challenge the universe at her side—a universe in which he prophetically sees "black holes in a fulgent sky" (319)—keeps Isabella informed, through his twelve letters, of the events connected with his own life. He writes of artistic and architectural accomplishments in Rome; of his friendship with Erasmus, author of a sensational book entitled *In Praise of Folly*; of Venice, France, and England; of the opposing stances between Martin Luther and Cardinal Wolsey; and of his distress at his King's defiance of the Pope to marry Anne Boleyn. "Kings grow and the collective spiritual force shrinks," he laments to Isabella, applauding Thomas More's "sublime battle" against Henry VIII (540).

De la Pole, the humanist, understands Erasmus's dilemma regarding the teachings of Luther, but is personally on the side of human civilization as the center of life: "We are on the side of the Ciceronians and the Virgilians, of the poets and artists who today are constructing the Christian Olympus: and Michelangelo and above all Raphael—how could they possibly be commissioned by a Luther?" (324).

Thus, the separate destinies of Isabella d'Este and Robert de la Pole are synchronized by the rhythm and span of his letters. The book closes with a short "Room of the Clocks" entry, as the precious timepieces sound their strokes in different tones and tempos, and the hourglass of Isabella's life slowly and quietly runs toward the end of its last measure.

Susanna Agnelli (see Chapter Seven, below) likewise reconstructs the life of a historical figure, Giuseppe Garibaldi, through an imaginary correspondence that conforms to the strict definition of the epistolary novel. *Ricordati Gualeguaychù* (Remember Gualeguaychù, 1982) is a sort of love song composed for the centenary of the death of Garibaldi, consisting of imaginary letters written by women who acclaim his "heroism of the two worlds."

Natalia Ginzburg's two epistolary novels, *Caro Michele* (*Dear Michael*, 1973, translated also as *No Way*) and *La città e la* *casa* (*The City and The House*, 1984), have a certain continuity between them, for the characters in both are similar and both novels deal with errors committed within family units of the bourgeois social class. Lack of real affection and of respect for institutions underlies the failures of the characters' "adult" marriages, "young" marriages, and "living together" arrangements. Separations are caused by sexual deviations, generation gaps, and cultural vacuums. Such is the stuff of Natalia Ginzburg's disheartening epistolary novels.

Dear Michael, a mixture of narrative in the third person singular and letters that express the impossibility of communication between mother and son, tells the story of the gradual social breakdown, after the industrial boom of the 1960s with its discomforting negative effects, among the members of a bourgeois Roman family of intellectuals—a unit that stands in direct contrast to the indissoluble group in *Family Sayings* (see Chapter Four, above). Michele of the title is a twenty-two-year-old artist and would-be terrorist, son of an unsuccessful but well-to-do, eccentric painter (separated from his wife, Michele's mother), who dies early in the novel. After a period of hippy existence on his own in a basement apartment, Michele begins his wanderings throughout Europe, experiencing a short, unhappy marriage to an alcoholic. His life of dissatisfaction ends early, when he is stabbed by a fascist in Bruxelles.

The movement and the dynamics of the letters are based on Michele's various voyages, which take on the symbolism of distance and emphasize the lack of contact among the characters. Assemblage of the personages is achieved only through letters, remarkable for their openness and accuracy of reportage but which fail dismally to knit the raveled family fabric. The many letters Michele's mother writes to him, and few of which he answers, produce the sound of a voice crying out in the desert. The difficulties of the decidedly unilateral dialogue of the deaf between mother and son are compounded by the fact that the letters rarely reach their destination, or inconveniently cross each other; thus the reader cannot help but feel that the missives are nothing but desperate, futile attempts to fill the void and break the silence which hold mother and son enthralled.

The City and The House likewise develops the themes of incommunicability, desperation and solitude. The characters in this novel write to friends, acquaintances, and members of the family, but actually they are writing to themselves for they know that all interpersonal attachments are artificial. They are apart from all human beings, in the company only of their own feelings of discomfort, wretchedness, or anger. Giuseppe, a fifty-year-old journalist, after leading a disordered love life, experiencing a quickly broken marriage and fathering two unloved children in Italy, without regret or remorse moves to America to live out his old age together with an elder brother. One of Giuseppe's sons, Alberico, is a homosexual and a would-be film star. After a period of hippy existence, he makes an attempt at setting up a pseudofamily with a homosexual friend, Salvatore, and a child-mother, Nadia, while Giuseppe, in America, becomes involved in a series of overpowering life, love, and death events involving his older brother's family. In Italy, all the members of Alberico's pseudofamily are killed by a gang of roughs. Giuseppe, now completely alone, toys with his memories and with the idea of returning to Italy. He finds no better interlocutor than himself, and no better vehicle of expression than his letters for his dramatic soliloquy.

Thus, important contemporary themes—loneliness, the impossibility of communication between young and old, the disintegration of the family structure, etc.—are effectively treated by Natalia Ginzburg in two novels of the epistolary genre.

An inventive construction is the one conceived by **Gianna Manzini** (see Chapter Four, above) in *Lettera all'editore* (Letter to the publisher, 1945), the whole novel consisting of the letter written by the author to her publisher outlining her novel-in-the-making, into which the plot and vivid character delineation are intricately woven, and personal matters, such as her nostalgia for Tuscan landscapes, all combine into a ready-made novel. *Lettera all'editore* must be seen, however, more as a literary document than as a novel, for it is an exposé of the limitations of certain literary models which the author considered inadequate to convey the impact of the realities of World War II. To this problem of artistic expression, Manzini, alone among women writers, sought to provide a satisfactory reply. Her *Lettera all'editore*, therefore, documents not only a personal writing crisis, but a juncture in Italian literature as well. She is the first to have intuited the neorealism that came to dominate the Italian literary scene after the war. Yet she was also the first to see that the trend could limit the art of prose, and indeed, by the 1950s, neorealism had fallen into a state of rigid conformism. She saw the necessity of going beyond it, to a literature of things, facts, and feelings that are *"impegnati"* (involved, *engagés*)— that is, a literature that would go beyond the chronicling of the quotidian and become a substitute for "*letteratura della memoria.*"

  Lettera all'editore is, then, a novel about a literary crisis, but it also recounts an adventure in which she is personally involved with her characters. She proposes a unique definition of the true novel: the conjoining of autobiography and plot in an inexorable exchange between author and character, which not only stirs up the stuff of personal memories, but undergoes constant revision by the friend and publisher who receives the "letter."

  Thus, the epistolary novel has proven itself to be, in the hands of Italian women authors, not just a vehicle for high-flown romantic sentiment, nor a work whose central characters are exemplary figures from the point of view of education and breeding. It is a modern, versatile, dynamic genre, technically suited to the inventiveness of writers whose works in progress are still in a phase of expansion.

Chapter Six

From Antifeminism to Feminism

"Feminists? In my vast reading public, there are none, and I'm glad. Once, in a feminist bookshop, there was a sign: 'No books by Liala for sale here': that's just fine, too bad for them."[1]

The majority of women writers at the turn of the century—Liala, Invernizio, Neera, Colombi, Vivanti—were, like most of their contemporaries, antifeminist and antidivorcist. Even the socially militant journalist, Matilde Serao (see Chapter Two, above) took a stand against women's suffrage and further declared that the only women who might benefit from divorce would be the wives of thieves and assassins.[2] As for her own extramarital relations and a daughter born out of wedlock, Serao kept well and truly silent.

Centering on female characters living out their lives for a female public, the so-called "popular romances" of the period focused on the intimate domain of women: family, children, servants, and gossip. Thus addressed, women enjoyed the attention paid to their sex in the popular romances, read also by working women who, having been freed from hand labor by the mechanization of industries, now had time to read. Many of them found consolation and escape in the romantic situations of girls of lowly condition becoming, thanks to their virtuousness, ladies of a higher class. The only end of every romance was marriage. Daydreaming heroines had but one desire: to nick an ideal marriage, have children, and enjoy security. Every wild joy or furious failure in all these romances hinges on the success or failure of clinching a good marriage.

Liala (Amalia Liana Cambiasi Negretti Odescalchi [1897-   ]) insists on this last recipe as the only one for happiness in over eighty "rosy" popular novels. Her protagonists struggle to acquire respectability and standing, channeling all their emotions, passions, and energies into building a decorous facade for themselves. Liala claims that good manners and mutual respect really are the secret of a successful marriage and that this is the subject matter she teaches. Although her novels were read mainly during the era of fascism, recent reeditions are not uncommon and, interestingly enough, *Chiamami con un altro nome* (Call me by another name, 1958, successive editions 1963, 1975, 1978, 1984) found its place on a bestseller list in Italy in February 1989. One critic explains Liala's success by the linearity of the story "as it should be": adherence to a few moral and social principles produces a "repose effect" essential for escapist literature, and the heroine falls easily into her saccharine roles.[3] Thus, the female reader who continues to depend on protection by the male is attracted to Liala's novels even today.

The even more prolific **Caterina Invernizio** (1858-1916), queen of Italian popular romances, provided continuing education for her countrywomen in the form of one hundred thirty sentimental, pathetic, and terrifying novels always on the subjects of sin, perdition, and crime. Written in a modern yet melodramatic style, the plethora of Invernizio's novels helped to fill the dreary emptiness of her readers' days. Her reading public was drawn from the entire social spectrum, and, in her books, whenever there arises the question of saving face, women of all classes close ranks.

Invernizio's women protagonists may be divided into sinners and saints, whose emotions are treated through description and dialogue with no attempt at psychological introspection.[4] Punishment is always meted out to seductresses and other transgressors, while reward is guaranteed to the woman who protects sacred family unity.

The popularity of both Liala and Invernizio was due probably to the fact that they gave their women readers more or less what they subconsciously sought, that is, a description of themselves.[5] The feminine models of both authors live in the closed world of public opinion; they accept the rules of the game and expend their energies fighting for family unity and respectability. But whereas male characters resolve intrigues with blood and sword, women achieve victory by scheming and artifice.[6]

Gradually, however, the established order of male dominance in the marriage institution begins to be questioned. The literary heroine manifests uneasiness in her surroundings, and the apparently happily married woman does, in fact, suffer secretly. Women protagonists, starting to feel the oppression of their daily existence, open their eyes to incompatibilities in human relationships and to the impossibility of attaining higher goals; and women writers accordingly awaken to the need of a *prise de conscience* regarding their problems. The novels of Matilde Serao, Grazia Deledda, Ada Negri, Sibilla Aleramo, Neera, Marchesa Colombi, Alba de Céspedes, and minor writers such as Cristina Trivulzio di Belgioioso (1808-1871) and Emma (Emilia Ferretti Villa, 1844-1929) attest to an even stronger will to denounce women's condition, protest against injustices, and demand the rights to education, the vote, and equal salary. Even the antifeministic Liala, after 1931, began to treat the theme of women's emancipation in her novels. Just when a measure of progress was apparently being made in this direction, however, fascism arrived on the scene to glorify the "mother/wife of Fascist soldiers" role (the so-called "angels of the hearth") and thereby stifle at the source women's search for autonomy.

In the development of this chapter, the chronological order of presentation of women novelists will coincide with the growth of feminine militancy up to the "revolution" of the late 1960s and the 1970s. Now, in the early 1990s, Italian women writers, less sex-conscious, less reticent to move away from participation in a collective feminist movement, are following a trend that permits them to affirm their individuality by detaching themselves from the organized activity of women's rights movements.

Neera (1846-1918), the pseudonym of Anna Radius Zuccari, is a self-styled antifeminist who, unlike Caterina Percoto whose writings were considered too realistic and masculine (see Chapter Two, above), churned out effusive "womanly" novels in which she exalts maternity and the domestic hearth. The *summa* of her antifeminism may be found in her book of essays entitled *Le idee di una donna* (A woman's ideas, 1903), in which she declares that George Eliot and George Sand gave little to humanity as compared to the obscure mothers of Leonardo da Vinci and Dante Alighieri. She actually claims that the greatest feminine achievement imaginable is mothering a just man.

Neera is convinced that the sexes are diverse and unequal. Her plots revolve around women's conflicts between desire and duty, between the call of the senses and the spirit of self-sacrifice. Her own ideals of perfect union between man and wife, and of Platonic love, both rest on a solid moral philosophy. Passionate

and meditative, writing in a style ranging from the lyrical to the
artificial, Neera practically exhausts the subject of women's biological creativity. Yet she is sensitive to women who lack maternal instinct and is wholly sympathetic towards disillusioned
wives. In *Teresa* (1886), where she recognizes that layers of taboos have been imposed with violence on women, the heroine
attempts to shed these outer shells and courageously find her
own identity without compromise. Although she finally succeeds in leaving her domestic surroundings and defying public
opinion, this is so out of Neeran character that the conclusion of
the book seems, according to more than one critic, quite implau-
sible.[7] Neera's heroines generally stand in deep contradiction to
themselves, outwardly conformist but inwardly dissatisfied.

L'*indomani* (The day after, 1890) best illustrates the theme
of the silent daily oppression of women. The just-married Marta
was raised and educated in the cult of male supremacy, dreaming of the knight in shining armor who would change her life
radically. After her first night with her husband, Alberto, her future expectation is that she will receive true love from him!
Marta rationalizes their first night of sexual relations as "right,
legal, approved by civil law and by religion" (11). She now has a
need for fusion with Alberto, which physical closeness had only
aroused without satisfying. As time passes, Marta begins to feel
out of place in her husband's home town, sensing that his past
stands between them. Glances between Alberto and his servant,
his loving caresses for his horse, his endless conversations with
men friends, give her the sensation of being excluded. She notes
that he calls his friends "dear" in the same tone as he calls her
"dear," and that he shies from her "indecorous" caresses when
they are in public.

Marta, however, needs these caresses. Outwardly she is
happy, but sometimes she is assailed by vague melancholy and
discouragement—for which she blames only herself. Gradually,
verbal communication between them ceases, and physical suffering sets in. She comes to realize that "*amore*," a word that in her
youth she thought would bring prodigious changes in her life,
actually had altered nothing and must therefore be an illusion.
Feeling no new sensations or vibrations, no new transports of
joy, she grows weak, nervous, irritable, and jealous, in the face of
Alberto's serene coldness and his long absences from home.
Marta falls victim to sensual hallucinations during which her
self-caresses exhaust her and cause her to become mentally paralyzed and physically rigid when at night her husband draws her

to him in bed. Pregnancy reduces her to a lackluster figure that finds no thrill in her imminent motherhood since she had known no thrill in the act of love.

Witnessing by chance a young country couple making passionate and tender love, she suddenly has a "revelation of another life, bursting into bloom with [the couple's] revelation of love" (133). To her mother, who has come to visit, Marta enthusiastically exclaims: "Love exists!"—after which they have a formal debate on illusion vs. reality. For Marta's mother, there do exist desire, dream, religion, and maternity—that is, love transformed—but love itself is an illusion. The final pages of the novel are a melodramatic tirade, entertaining for the modern reader, in which Marta concludes that since love and truth do exist, women must continue to search for them.

Neera expresses, in *L'indomani*, the distastefulness of marital constraint and intimacy that Marta comes to hate, but finally sublimates it by attaching sentimental importance to the biological phenomenon that is her unborn baby. *L'indomani* is not yet a clearly stated *prise de conscience* regarding woman's conditioning by her environment and of society's imposition of taboos, but the reader nevertheless acutely feels the wife's discomfort diffused throughout the book.

Whereas Marta lacks the self-assurance that earns women their triumphs and conquests, the superiority of the beautiful, intelligent Lilia of *Una passione* (*A Passion*, 1903), is proclaimed throughout the entire novel by her suitors and admirers. She is one of those rare women, like Madame de Staël's Corinne, who know how to love and make themselves loved. Sensitively described by Neera, Lilia, in her natural geniality, appears like a dreamlike creature surrounded by flatterers and pretendants who ascribe to her the characteristics of a delicate flower and an ungraspable ray of light (19-20). None of her suitors, however, succeeds in pleasing Lilia; instead, she enters into a passionate liaison with young Ippolito, an undomesticated orphan, now specializing in organ music at the conservatory of Bergamo. Early in the novel, learning that Ippolito is striving to create a great organ composition, the reader can anticipate that it will be Lilia's inspiration that will carry him through.

Conversation in Lilia's salon revolves around the moral dictum: "if it is true that the world is sunk in a mire of vice, it is also true that the heights exist. And that is where one must take refuge" (157). The maxim sets the tone for Lilia's and Ippolito's efforts to reach greater heights through art and creative pursuits.

Symbiosis is, however, inevitable and thus is born a passion that transforms soul and senses. Whereas Ippolito's is all-consuming, Lilia's is cerebral (164). She finds Ippolito refreshingly different from the habitués of her salon, but she is not prepared to sacrifice her life style for him. Both Ippolito and Lilia, however, are now moving toward "a form of love as close as possible to perfection" (217).

The huge success of Ippolito's original organ composition reassures Lilia of her faith in art. Ippolito accompanies Lilia to Bellagio on Lake Como, where the couple spend a month of such intense closeness that Neera is obliged to use the traditional dotted line to replace omitted physical love scenes. Suddenly, Lilia's past looms, forming a wall between the two. The real world crowds out their voluptuous isolation when Lilia notices Ippolito's enthusiasm for a family and its baby living in a nearby villa. Lilia well knows Ippolito's craving for a family—which had been denied him—and his former simple childhood life, but her own past precludes this choice for herself. Now is the moment for Neera to push her antifeminism: Ippolito's desire for a wife and children is more natural than Lilia's lack of maternal instinct. Lilia who, according to Neera, does not truly love because she reasons, drives the young man to the brink of madness, but his art will save him. She convinces him that the role of art is to create and render the creator immortal, that she will die but Ippolito's glory will live on forever. "All her past glories seem to be dust in comparison with the superhumanness of that hour" (385) is the closing sentence of the novel.

Lilia seems to have known *a priori* what Marta in *L'indomani* did not recognize: that past attachments keep the married man and woman apart. Romantic love, Neera tells the reader in both novels, is an illusion. Both Marta and Ippolito suffer because they cannot achieve the fusion they seek with their mates, but they both dream of another kind of ideal love. For Marta, it will take the form of Maternity; for Ippolito, Art. Speaking of matrimony as a condition that gives meaning to life, Neera is, then, referring to an ideal, because the real image, as seen in both *L'indomani* and *A Passion*, implies emptiness and depersonalization.

The heroines of the novels of **Marchesa Colombi**[8] (1846-1920), pseudonym of Maria Antonietta Torelli-Vollier (or Torriani), are similar to those of Neera: they are suffocated by life's monotony. Both have an unspoken, rancorous, repressed consciousness of the enslavement of women,[9] but whereas Neera proclaimed her antifeminism, Colombi involved herself, from as early as 1870, in Lombardy's feminist activity. The movement had its roots in the writings of **Cristina Trivulzio di Belgioioso** (especially *Della presente condizione delle donne e del loro avvenire*, On the present condition of women and their future, 1866), and of **Emma**, author of *Una fra tante* (One among many, 1878), a book on prostitution that created a scandal at the time of its publication and has recently been reedited with a preface by Italy's outstanding feminist, Dacia Maraini (see below).

One of Colombi's most important works is *In risaia* (In the rice paddies, 1878), which treats the problems of the hardships and privations of peasant women and of the apathetically resigned proletariat. The subject is handled in a nonidyllic, ironic manner: Nanna, working in the putrid waters of the mosquito-breeding fields of Lombardy, dreams of earning the money required to buy the traditional silver hair ornament worn by brides of the region. The entire verbal portrait of Nanna is drawn in the past conditional: she "could have been very beautiful," "could have had marvelous hair," etc. if only poverty had not forced her to work in the freezing cold and oppressive heat of the rice paddies. Nanna patiently puts aside the few lire she earns each day, continuing to work even though affected by debilitating swamp fever—until one day she learns of more profitable labor: exposing her legs to leeches that attach themselves to the flesh to draw blood, permitting her to catch them, put them into jars, and sell them to the local pharmacy for a higher price than her workday. Lending her already macerated legs to this new endeavor, Nanna contracts typhoid fever, diagnosed by a local witch doctor as "cephalitis," for which the infallible cure was capping the head of the patient with a freshly slaughtered black chicken. The delirious Nanna is finally taken to the hospital, where the nurses, attempting to remove from her head the coagulated blood and putrefied visceral juices of the chicken, inflict terrible pain on her. During her six months of illness and convalescence, Nanna develops a scalp infection that leaves her head—which was to be crowned with a silver hair ornament—"bald and shiny like a knee."

The gray Lombardy plains of *In risaia*, whose waters are infested with insects, worms, and leeches, are symbolic of the relentless clutch of poverty and the tedium of daily existence. Colombi's 1885 novel, *Un matrimonio in provincia* (A country wedding) is likewise set in a hostile northern region—Piedmont—in the grim, silent town of Novara where the heroine,

the generous and naïve Denza, suffers an ironic fate similar to
that of Nanna. The novel, which may be read at a sitting, and
which leaves the reader with the most vivid of impressions as
pointed out by Natalia Ginzburg in her introduction to the 1973
edition, revolves around a young woman in a critical relationship with her society and its institutions, in particular marriage.
Denza is the younger daughter of a notary, whose modest family
lives a Spartan existence. Although a natural beauty, her stepmother stifles her until the betrothal of Denza's older sister,
Titina. Accordingly, Denza must dress poorly and wear a bun.
Her hands are swollen with chilblains and she is forced to care
for the baby that is born to her stepmother, which makes her a
grotesque figure as she walks through the town with the baby
clinging to her neck. The simple fact that an obese young man of
a well-to-do family happened to look at her with interest leads
Denza straight to her looking glass. Beginning now to concern
herself with her appearance, she daydreams about her future life
with the ponderous young Onorato Mazzucchetti, who, at their
first direct contact, looked longingly at her and uttered a few ar-
dent words. The proud and happy Denza, industriously building
her castles in Spain, imagines herself officially engaged and soon
to be married to the "elephant" whom she loves passionately—
only because he had looked at her and made her happy. Onorato, however, has been sent by his parents for a visit to the Paris
Exposition followed by a long trip through Europe, while Denza
waits long, empty, monotonous months until his return. Her
wait is in vain: in a brutal manner she learns that Onorato is engaged to another young woman solely for her dowry. Denza's
disillusionment is paroxysmal. A melancholy and pathetic figure, she now imagines herself the laughing stock of Novara,
which she would like to leave either by entering a convent or
simply by dying of shame.

The old maid Denza is now twenty-six years old. Her sister, Titina, and her other women cousins have all married,
while she, the prettiest of them all, is left without a husband! So
abjectly dull is her existence that she accepts an arranged marriage with an older man, a landed notary. All she knows about
him is that he has a large wart on his right temple. Denza, still
entertaining sentimental illusions, accepts. At their first encounter, she yearns to hear words of love from him, but instead
he describes the workers' hygienic conditions in his rice fields
(the theme of *In risaia*) and tells her that, as his wife, she will
have to assist him in supervising the peasants' conditions: "I

was disheartened, because in the presence of that matter-of-fact man and in the fog of his rice paddies I saw vanish into thin air all my sentimental dreams. But I was resolved to marry him just so I wouldn't remain an old maid" (98-99). In the last seven lines of the novel, without transition from the marriage ceremony, the reader learns that Denza has three children and is growing fat. Obviously, she is comfortably married, but whether she is happy or not with the husband and his rice fields does not seem to be important. What is important is that she exists in a state of wedlock.

Thus, Neera's and Colombi's heroines play out silently the dramas of their eventless existences as frustrated housewives or young women living a life of restriction and boredom, pitilessly described. One critic has seen the novels of these two authors as counterparts of texts such as Charlotte Brontë's *Jane Eyre* (1847) and Louisa May Alcott's *Little Women* (1868), in that they teach girls the need to subordinate their individuality and will to others in order to become good wives and mothers through acquiescence, chastity, and self-sacrifice. Such socially conservative novels offer models for "growing down" rather than "growing up."[10]

The colorful figure of **Annie Vivanti** (1868-1942), poet and novelist whose name is intimately connected with the figure of Giosuè Carducci, is the author of works that enchanted the famous critic and philosopher, Benedetto Croce. Vivanti was born in London of an Italian Carbonarist father and a German mother, one of whose brothers, a poet, was a friend and lover of George Sand. Annie Vivanti's notable success as a writer in Italy, where she took up residence in 1887, did not spare her from social snubbing because she was both an Englishwoman and a Jewess. She died in Turin, forsaken and poverty-stricken, not long after receiving news of the death of her talented and beloved daughter and son-in-law in a London bombing during World War II.[11]

Like her lesser known contemporaries, **Amalia Guglielminetti** (1885-194?), **Clarice Tartufari** (1868-1933), and **Carola Prosperi** (1883- ?), Vivanti approaches the problems of the modern woman in her everyday life in a male-dominated society. The four novelists seek to pinpoint the unvoiced, elusive malaise that characterized Neera's and Colombi's heroines by explaining the societal reasons for women's feelings of disaffection and alienation. They set their estranged protagonists on the track of family vocation, however, thus illustrating their own retrogressive social views.

Vivanti's novel of almost four hundred pages, *I divoratori* (1911), first published in London in 1910 as *The Devourers*, brands her as an antifeminist, for in it she raises a monument to maternity as the exclusive justification for a woman's life.[12] The entire book revolves, in fact, around the conflict between sacrificial maternal love and women's self-realization, the stand taken by Vivanti being, of course, that the individuality of the mothers involved must be subordinated to society's overriding requirements.

The devourers of the title refer to children in general—especially children of an exceptionally talented mother—and, in particular, to the only child (daughter) of such a mother. Each gifted mother in the novel has a single child, a daughter, perforce a prodigy. The mother fatally renounces her own self-assertion, sacrificing herself in favor of the child, plucking one by one the feathers from her own wings to give free flight to the daughter, who then proceeds to devour her own mother.[13] The devouring daughters in their turn become talented mothers, who renounce love, genius, or immortality, capitulating to the call of nature and society, which demands of the protagonists reproduction, maternity, and submission to the protection of their bulwark husbands.

Other novels by Vivanti worthy of mention are the partly autobiographical *Marion* (her pseudonym at the time was George Marion), in which the heroine, a young cabaret singer, achieves her liberation as an artist and woman by committing a crime; the 1927 revised, "expurgated" version of the 1891 novel, however, took on an antifeminist slant: Marion, victimized by her two "macho" lovers, is reduced to an impersonalized life that is incompatible with her ideals of love and complete womanhood.

Vae Victis! (Latin for Woe to the conquered!, 1918) relates the tragic plight of girls raped during World War I. One of these victims, Ma Chérie, bears the unwanted child of "shame, violence, and pain" (369), thus becoming a suffering, guilt-ridden heroine in the temple of sanctifying Maternity. The plot of *Naja Tripudians* (Latin for Egyptian cobra, 1921), on the same theme of violated innocence, revolves around the debauching by London aristocrats of two innocent, naïve, teen-aged sisters from an English country village. The wicked Londoners' drinking, drugs, dissipation, and transvestism are menacingly described by

Vivanti, who, once again, strengthens the myth of feminine weakness and fragility and exhorts her women readers to toe the straight and narrow path. Vivanti skirts the real problem of male abuse, subordinating this feminist theme to fit the thesis of maternity and family as desirable vocations.[14] She dares to suggest that the end justifies the means: that since the woman is now a respectable mother, all is well!

The desirability of the family vocation for the woman is posited also by **Gina Lagorio** (1930-   ), a post-World War II writer, whose short novel *Un ciclone chiamato Titti* (A cyclone named Titti, 1969) relates the unexpected advent of a child that disrupts the rhythm of a couple's life, but is ultimately considered an enrichment of it. The presence of the child in the household implies better understanding and a better future for the couple—a message that smacks of moralizing, as does that of *Approssimato per difetto* (More than estimated, 1971), in which Lagorio suggests that love and solidarity being one's only anchor of salvation, one must be vigilant in keeping one's marriage ever wakeful and symbiotic. Likewise, in *Fuori scena* (Offstage, 1979), with its obvious religious overtones,[15] the heroine intimates that perhaps woman alone can bring hope and renewal to the earth by suggesting a way of life that is "more human because maternal" (218). Absence of warmth and friendship makes for a woman's utter hopelessness and despair in *Tosca dei gatti* (Tosca of the cats, 1983), while in *Golfo del paradiso* (Gulf of paradise, 1987), feminist themes[16] are buried under the plot—a search for a lost painting—into which passages on art and art criticism are artificially inserted, and the last part of the book is heavily weighted with esthetic and metaphysical considerations.

The strong moralistic overtones of Lagorio's works, and her emphasis on maternity as "the only acceptable way of filling one's role as an actor on stage and not a spectator" (*Un ciclone chiamato Titti*, 88), bring the reader almost full swing back to Liala, Neera, and their cortege of antifeminists.

The realistic portrayal of women's problems and of their revolt was the aim of feminist authors, who chose for their writings a style that not only would describe the social and economic grievances harbored by their sex but would alter ingrained perceptions of woman's inferiority and objectification. Committed to analyzing themselves and their role in a conventional society, feminist women writers were determined to correct in some measure the injustices that were so deeply rooted in Italian cultural and religious traditions. Two early twentieth-century authors, well known in the Italian feminist movement for having brought women's issues to the political and historical fore, are **Camilla Ravera** (see Chapter Seven, below) and **Iris Origo** (1902-1988). Writing mainly in English since she was born in England of an Irish nobelwoman and a wealthy American father, Iris Origo lived with her husband, the marchese Antonio Origo, in Tuscany at Val d'Orcia (where she took part in the wartime struggle of the partisans) in the villa "La Foce" frequented by intellectuals of the ilk of Bernard Berenson, D.H. Lawrence, and Gordon Craig. Like Anna Banti and Maria Bellonci (q.v.), Origo used Italian Renaissance civilization as material for her literary production, while feminist issues found expression in her personal souvenirs contained in an autobiography, *Immagini e ombre* (Images and Shadows, published in England, 1970, Italian translation, 1984) as well as in pen portraits of Ruth Draper and others.

It is **Sibilla Aleramo** (1876-1960), however, who must be considered Italy's first true feminist; it is she who dominates from the top rung of the feminist literary ladder of her time, having produced a formidable assemblage of works with feminist themes and socio-political theses; and it is her novel, *Una donna* (*A Woman*, 1906), on which early twentieth-century feminism hinges. Sibilla Aleramo (pseudonym of Rina Pierangeli Faccio) lived in her own person the anguish of the female condition. Generous and defenseless, exposed to the dangers and deceits of the double moral standards with which men—even writers and poets[17]—settle affairs of the heart, she courageously refused all conventions. She was an eclectic poet and novelist with a deep social sensitivity that involved her, according to Italy's changing political tides, first as a socialist, then as a fascist, and finally as a militant communist. Her wide social commitments extended to the creation and management of schools, social assistance centers, and dispensaries in the Roman and Pontine plains. At the same time, her private life was tormented and tempestuous. Amorously linked to persons of both sexes, her artistic and cultural growth was favorably influenced by the extraordinary gamut of stirring human and amorous relationships she entertained; those very liaisons, however, were to heap blame on her person and stir bitterness in her soul.

Aleramo became the principal model for women writing between the two world wars, and authors such as Fausta Cialente and Gianna Manzini (q.v.) considered her their most authoritative predecessor. *A Woman*, begun in 1902 and published four

years later, is an autobiographical and prophetic "novel of conscience," which Aleramo herself described as containing the best
of her spirit and the most of her own future.[18] The novel analyzes the intense life experience, travailed by mounting personal
and social problems, of a prototypic woman associable with Ev-
erywoman.[19] The vital, intelligent, passionate woman vigorously defends her dignity and her inalienable right to play a role
in the life of the community, but at the cost of a devastating rejection of her marriage and maternity.

Disillusioned first by the base conduct of her father whom
she had loved and admired, and then by her ambitious, avid,
sensual, and vulgar husband who had married her only after
having raped her in her father's office, the protagonist is
doomed to a life of reclusion in a small, stifling southern town
devoid of culture. The novel gives the best sense of the home as
a place of confinement and alienation for the superior woman,
who is neither recognized nor understood by her community.
Driven to the brink of suicide by her husband's jealousy, forced
to make the difficult choice between home and child, or becoming her own person, she decides to seek wider horizons in the
world of ideas, books, and journalism, which she had experienced briefly in Rome when her husband had "allowed" her to
work because of their economic difficulties. She is determined
now to affirm her own identify and to participate in the "ideal
construction of a world"—a mission that will make up for the
insufficiency of her wifely state. She refuses sex as a violent and
passive subjection of women to masculine desire; she refuses
subjugation to the "maternal function"; she wills the destruction
of a highly resistant feminine model; and, by indicating new
paths in the mother-son relationship, she exorcises the maternal
mystique.[20]

Considered a landmark in the battle for equality of the
sexes and women's liberation, Aleramo's *A Woman* has been
reprinted many times in Italy. In its 1977 edition (Milano: Feltrinelli), a preface by critic Maria Antonietta Macciocchi (see
Chapter Seven, below) further praises the novel as a powerful
weapon—in a rigorously Marxist ideological context—for the
battle against bourgeois moral hegemony.[21] Specialized criticism
has unjustly assigned Aleramo to the ranks of minor writers, but
her intellectual vitality as well as her links with the world of culture of her time make her an important figure in any panorama
of Italian literature. Moreover, the extraordinary way in which
Aleramo constructs the portrait of "a woman" turns out to be a

mirror of her own "myth of self." The mirror reflects a particular idea of life that had guided all of her choices: to live, for her,
meant to be necessary to another person; without this necessity,
one simply exists—a thought that goes far in reordering the
complex relationships between woman and man, woman and
child, and woman and woman in both Aleramo's and her
readers' own world.

The myth of self also underlies novels by **Alba de Céspedes** (1911-　, see Chapter Four, above), an Italian by birth and
by marriage, but of Cuban origin. (She is the granddaughter of
Carlos Manuel de Céspedes, the liberator and first president of
Cuba, and the daughter of a later Cuban president.) Although
characterized by one critic as the author of "feminine bourgeois
psychological novels,"[22] de Céspedes repeatedly returns to the
theme of the rights of women in marriage—especially their spiritual and intellectual rights—and in a vigorous, elegant style she
anticipates by several years the upcoming debate in Italy of the
condition of women in family and society.

De Céspedes studies the relationship between the psychology of a woman and her environment. Her wives seek from
their husbands comradeship, respect as individuals, and sup-
portive interest in their activities. They will not make conces-
sions, even at the price of their personal happiness. *Quaderno
proibito* (Forbidden notebook, 1952, translated as *The Secret*)[23]
and the novella, *Prima e dopo* (*Between Then and Now*, 1955),
each in its own way examines the dilemma of a woman who desires to be a wife and mother but also an individual in her own
right. Whether or not she is successful in her struggle for complete emancipation, she finds that the price of self-realization is
loneliness and isolation.

Forbidden Notebook relates the story of a middle-class
married working woman, Valeria Cossati, mother of two children, in an intriguing secret search for her own identity. She
does all the household chores, which leaves her with a sense of
futility, while her husband and son belittle her secretarial work
at her office. Some unconscious impulse prompts Valeria to buy
a black notebook that is to become her secret diary and which she
will frantically search to keep hidden from her husband and
children. Initially a simple record of events and feelings, the secret diary, written with the pen of Alba de Céspedes, grows into a
painful confession of a forty-three-year-old woman living
through the crumbling of a traditional marriage-and-family
structure and an unresolved love for her employer, Guido—

unresolved because she lives it out through her family, without allowing either herself or Guido the freedom and happiness lovers deserve. The genuineness of Valeria's feelings for Guido are tempered by family considerations and frustrations, for she knows of the contrasts and contradictions inherent in the image of what Valeria Cossati "should be" for her family, for Guido, and for herself. The split in Valeria's personality and in her desires, when her duties at the office clash with her obligations at home, produce a torment that may be compared to that of the legendary Iseult, victim of a love potion: unable to find peace at home, Valeria runs to the office to be with Guido; when she is at the office, her every happy gesture is weighed down by guilt, and she yearns to return to the protection of her home.

Although her husband, Michele, and her son, Riccardo, are content with the external manifestations of Valeria, her twenty-year-old daughter, Mirella, refusing to accept surface images, is in constant conflict with her mother. Valeria recognizes that she herself may be at fault, that she may be envious of her daughter's free life style, and is frustrated by the fact that she has ceased to be a model for her daughter. She realizes that she scarcely knows Mirella at all, nor can ever be her friend, even after twenty years of care and devotion. She confides to her diary that there is much more understanding between herself and her elderly, rather cold and distant mother, than between Valeria and the "revolutionary" Mirella, and in the pages devoted to her emotional meanderings in search of her own mother and her own daughter, the reader is made privy to the importance for Valeria of writing as a form of communication and understanding. Like that of the narrator in Fausta Cialente's *Le quattro ragazze Wieselberger*, Valeria's setting of words on paper is an outlet, a form of self-expression, and a communications link as well.

Some of the most penetrating pages in the diary, from a psychological point of view, are Valeria's probings into herself and her inability to decipher why, to be the person she thinks she is, she has to be in contact with her husband and children. Her nightmares stem from conflict between what she wants to be and what she has to do and be. When she ventures out alone into the streets of her city, she feels disconcerted—which shows how solidly coated she is with fixed traditional role-playing habits. She has the clear sensation that she is tied to all the members of her family, without belonging to any of them. Pathetic is Valeria's conviction that a woman must always belong (rather than be necessary) to someone in order to be happy.

New zest for life enters Valeria's existence as the innocent notebook gradually becomes a powerful genie or evil spirit; she goes to it secretly late at night, as if to a lover; it assumes gigantic proportions of intrigue and conveys a sense of guilt. At times, her rendezvous seems to be a dialogue with the devil. With an increasing sense of urgency, Valeria keeps her tryst each day, hiding her few moments of writing pleasure from her family, fearing the loss of her "reputation" as a dedicated wife and mother. On the days she is afraid to face life, she neglects her writing, so the diary may be seen as an instrument for intermittent injections of courage into her flagging spirits. The pressing need for moments of escape are uncannily transferred to the reader of *Forbidden Notebook*, who, losing his/her own sense of reality, stealthily participates in Valeria's continual search for a safe hiding place for the diary: the rag bag, the kitchen draw, or behind the ironing board, anywhere! Valeria has no "room of her own." Each time she helps the notebook abscond, she blushes, for she cannot understand that she has done nothing wrong.

What are the reasons for Valeria's determination to keep a diary? "I think I've reached the point where I must sum up my life, somewhat like putting order into a drawer into which I've thrown everything haphazardly for a long time" (67). Her disheartening summary, however, will amount to nothing more than the realization that life consists of good and bad, just and unjust, eternal and perishable values. Although she understands the importance of recording her inner feelings, Valeria is none the happier for having done so. Through self-analysis, she uncovers her own self-contradictions in a slow process of "know thyself." Doubts begin to arise; she nourishes them with bewilderment. She had been brought up without ideas of her own, morality having been learned as a child or dictated by her husband. Good and evil are elusive concepts, and what she used to think was solid has now lost consistency. What was cherished by her generation and that of her parents seem to have no worth for her children's generation, which values money and money only: her daughter Mirella freely accepts lavish gifts from a wealthy older suitor and her son, Riccardo, is determined to emigrate to Argentina in the hope of making a fortune there.

Giving in to her fears, Valeria ultimately resigns from her job to play the role of grandmother-babysitter to her son's child. To avoid making choices, she comes in out of the cold to the traditional hearth where all is preordained and preestablished. On the very last page of the novel, Valeria admits that she has no other desire than to leave her family and go off with Guido—a desire she has renounced for lack of courage, or for what Mirella calls hypocrisy. Valeria's days henceforth will be, like the pages of her notebook, white, smooth, cold, like "slabs of tombstone." Circulating in the air is a slight odor emanating from the burning diary—representing Valeria's sacrifice and the symbolic death of her inner self.

Even though Valeria is the principal character of the novel, and her friend, Clara, a successful script writer, is her alter ego, it is the young Mirella who is the novel's feminist heroine.[24] She is the only character who lives out completely her problems and her aspirations in a search for self-respect. She forces her family to alter the way of judging her behavior. In her work, she finds the completeness of her identity; in her love affair she combines not only sexual and sentimental affinities but above all a capacity for common intellectual interests and genuine communication with her partner. She has none of the feminine guilt feelings that plague Valeria. Only Mirella will find happiness because she has the courage to break traditional and conventional schemes to verify new patterns of life, to assert her rights, and to avoid being drawn into her mother's dilemma. The gist of Mirella's protest against her mother's subservience to the family is precisely what incites Valeria to keep her forbidden diary, so the young Mirella in essence knows *a priori* the "secret" her mother strives to keep.

Although the male figures in the novel lie in shadow and are not clearly delineated, the feminine triad—Valeria, her stiff-necked mother, and her rebellious daughter—provide a stunning example of the possibility of moving families an iota closer to the far-off noosphere, from one generation to the next.

A prolongation (and maturation) of Mirella is the courageous journalist, Irene, the protagonist of de Céspedes's 1955 novella, *Between Then and Now*. Mirella's budding iconoclasm within the bosom of the family from which she seeks escape is here lived out by Irene who, having experienced a generational as well as a socio-political gap with her family and society, has detached herself from her wealthy parents and fiancé, choosing to live alone in a quiet apartment that gives her "a pleasant impression of absolute freedom" (83). Irene's is a form of rebellion against conventional sham, and a battle for the supremacy of her "reason." As soon as she had taken on her own identity as a politically involved woman, her fiancé broke their engagement because she no longer fit the model of his traditional expectations. Irene has no sense of guilt or sin; no voice echoes in her ears that "it's forbidden." She is determined to live out her life style in its entirety and completeness, even though sometimes her "cursed life," her mania for reasoning, and her existential nausea bring her close to breaking under a weight she yearns to transfer to someone else's shoulders. At those moments, however, the necessity of "reasoning" suddenly reasserts itself and she returns to her original determination to retain independence and self-identity.

Irene, like Valeria in *Forbidden Notebook*, has reached the point when an apparently casual occurrence—the chance factor that offers a choice and divides time into "then" and "now"—prompts her to "sum up her life." Having left the traditional world of conformity—the "then" of the title—she is in search of a personal, inner freedom which she thought would bring happiness. Other persons in her entourage—Pietro, her lover; Erminia, her maid who has just resigned; Adriana, her closest friend—faced with similar conflicts, represent the clash between past and present. Those who gave up the happy unawareness of "then" do not succeed "now" in finding happiness and, in fact, fearing they represent enemies of dream and illusion, become a continuous threat to the happiness of others. This fear is to bring Irene and Pietro to the crucial point in their life and their love.

The three central figures—Irene, Pietro, and Adriana—have developed among themselves a harmonious relationship: "neither men nor women; we had learned to be simply human beings, equal; but our victory assumed—in the eyes of others—the aspect of defeat or guilt" (28). Musing on the meaning of the word "dignity," Irene recognizes that her life—like Pietro's or like Adriana's—instead of being "dignified" might be considered "*manquée*." All three of them are waiting for something, hoping for something in the future, instead of enjoying the present. During her work for the clandestine press in the South during the war, she had aspired to an ideal paradise on earth; after the war, she worked fanatically in search of a happiness which she felt, in her conscience, she deserved, but this happiness was illusory. The three central characters are aware they are living in an era of precariousness. They feel old because their lives contain a century of history; they would like to stop in their own epoch, but their epoch is precisely the weight of our times: "we always felt around us a presentiment of the end, and, at the same time, of the beginning; and often it seemed to us that we were still living as before, even though now it was after" (106-07). Even though they tried to enjoy the materialism and frivolity of the booming postwar economy, to them it seemed like an "extinguished firefly." So Irene's renunciation of a facile, bourgeois life, she sums up, was to create a "dignity" based on pride (*orgoglio*)—a sin of which she has always been guilty (110).

Irene needs to feel challenged; Pietro has too much faith in her, so her professional successes are not completely satisfying: "only for those who doubt our ability do we become satisfied if we succeed" (83). The tormenting question of the definition of love only increases her solitude and dismay, because she understands that each one, through his senses and his mind, by loving his partner, loves him/herself. Her considerations on the failure of love relationships lead her to contemplate Pietro lying on the bed beside her: "His body was thin, flat, on the surface of the bed, like a bas relief in a church pavement" (124). Irene wonders whether we are not all like stones on which names are engraved, over which people walk distractedly, gradually effacing with their footsteps the names inscribed—a simile comparable to the diary pages in *Forbidden Notebook*. She wonders about the usefulness of choosing one life style as opposed to another, whether to combat society or submit to it. She fears she has been behaving like a judge, trying to discern the guilt of others even while forgetting her own. She finally lies down next to Pietro, who looks at her uncertainly, as though they were both lost in a forest of stone and had to accept their human solitude (125). Taking him into her arms, she is overwhelmed by the desperation in which she has finally learned to recognize happiness. De Céspedes's message is that one must understand the relativity of the concept of happiness—that accepting it in its watered down form, one small happiness makes for another, as illustrated by the final, opportune telephone call from Adriana announcing to Irene that her maid, Erminia, is returning to her service.

Irene's sister, Marta, served during the war as a Red Cross nurse in Naples, where Irene, working for the underground press, frequently went to lend assistance to the sick and wounded. Although tired, the two sisters' capacity for work seemed unbounded. Never complaining, helping each other freely without hindthought, "there was something new between us: we were no longer sisters. Or at least we no longer felt an obligation to love each other, nor did we even love each other in the same sense as before . . . I no longer felt any blood ties to anyone" (64). This is another meaning of the title of the book: Irene "then" was caught up in a conventional sisterly relationship; "now" the two sisters, working together on behalf of freedom and humanity, helping out during air raids, have found a higher cause than family bonds. Irene and Marta share a mutual fear that something may happen to the other to prevent her from enjoying the dreamed-of postwar happiness, and each of the sisters finds her own happiness in this new relationship that goes beyond mere consanguine ties.

The only happiness attainable, Alba de Céspedes maintains, the only happiness to which one can aspire, is that of understanding. Irene has understood that her choice in life lay between pride and other less serious sins (110), and in this understanding she finds a feminine dignity and nobility that make her one of de Céspedes's most vigorous and unforgettable figures.

Contemporaries of Sibilla Aleramo, writing in the early twentieth century, had polished varied facets of the pens of feminists: **Maria Messina** (Chapter Two, above) described the tragedy implicit in the lives of women constrained to live in silence and reclusion in their tightly shuttered homes in Italy's deep South, and **Ada Negri**, as has been seen (Chapter Four, above), emphasized woman's double enslavement by her employer and her husband. A half century later, during the 1970s, the theme of women's marginality and their socio-economic inferiority continued to be pertinaciously treated in Italian women's writings. **Giuliana Ferri**, author of *Un quarto di donna* (A quarter of a woman, 1973), lends a title to her novel that underlines the extreme violence done to the tortured body and soul of the protagonist who dangles painfully between the public work life that has been made available to her (her extrahousehold identity) and the wife/mother private life that requires her to play a basic affective-expressive role (her family identity);[25] thus she is pulled in several directions and savagely torn into parts. **Gabriella Magrini**, in *Lunga giovinezza* (Long youth, 1976), denounces the exclusion of women from a personalized social and productive life, and focuses on the segregated role of the woman in the context of the married couple.[26] **Carla Cerati**'s novel, *La condizione sentimentale* (Sentimental condition, 1977) tells of a possessive love outside the regular institution of marriage, but which nevertheless binds a woman so tightly that her public and private personalities are split and she is denied the wholeness of

her psyche.[27] **Armanda Guiducci** theorizes on a similar profound dichotomy in *La mela e il serpente* (The apple and the
snake, 1974), subtitled "A woman's self-analysis," while her cultural history of women as bought commodities in the market-
place is entitled *Donna e serva* (Woman and servant, 1983). In
two, dry, penetrating household inquests, Guiducci contemplates
couples in their marital exasperation: *Due donne da buttare*
(Two disposable women, 1976)[28] and *La donna non è gente*
(Women aren't people, 1977); and her first novel, *A testa in giù*
(Decapitation, 1984), is the story of a woman's experience of psy-
chic oppression in the name of love.

The difficulty of breaking loose from the historical limitations imposed on women—limitations fashioned by time
over aeons and so deeply encrusted that the overlay seems in-
herently natural—is exquisitely captured by **Francesca Sanvitale**
(1928-   ), a contemporary woman writer very much in the
public eye. (Her most recent novel, *Verso Paola*, was in the
running for the Comisso Prize in 1991.) Sanvitale's first novel,
Il cuore borghese (Middle-class heart, 1972), is a complex work
interweaving elements of realism, hermetism, oneirism, and
techniques of the *école du regard*. It is a *catalogue raisonné* of
masculine and feminine middle-class behavior patterns,
systematically applied to the ancient gods, and contains as well
some rudiments of feminist themes. Sanvitale's best-known
novel, however, is *Madre e figlia* (Mother and daughter, 1980),
tracing the pilgrimage to alien lands of a strong and mature
child, Sonia, and her weak, irresponsible, still somewhat
childlike mother, Marianna. Told in the timeless-spaceless
dimension of a fable, the novel leads the reader on a double path
through Sonia's childhood, adolescence, and adulthood, and
through Marianna's youth up to the year following her death.
The tale is told in the first person singular, seemingly by Sonia,
but as she narrates, she becomes a character in the story; rarely,
however, does she reveal her age or her appearance at any given
time. Her inner self flashes back and forth in the story as if it
were her soul, speaking and dreaming in nonlinear time.

The mother's weak character arouses the compassion and
solidarity of her daughter, who loves the rich, noble family of
Marianna's past and imagines the charm of their turn-of-the-
century world. After the first world war, however, Marianna is
faced with facts and not fantasy.

Her father had died when she was thirty years of age but
still an adolescent and wholly defenseless. Left to face the world

without any solid foundations or value judgments, and a "bit stupid," Marianna surrenders herself in operatic fashion to a handsome but already married cavalry officer, who had appeared to her on his steed out of the dark night, wrapped her in his billowing military cape, and declared his abiding love for her—a love that was to last, however, only until she became pregnant, after which Marianna and her baby daughter, Sonia, are abandoned by the handsome officer. Here begins the miserable, lonely, humiliating existence of mother and daughter, who wander from city to city, living in ever poorer furnished rooms as the father becomes ever more indifferent and cruel.

It is precisely this maltreated Sonia who opens her heart to her reader with all her poetic capacity to dream, imagine, and transform. (This parallels Elisa's magic workings in Elsa Morante's *House of Liars* [see Chapter Four, above].) In the rectangle of luminous sky that Sonia sees through her window as she lies on the dirty bed of her room in the lowly quarters of Rome, the strident black lines that slash the blue square are long-winged swallows that cut through her immobility, rousing within her a pure force that will compel her forward in her pilgrimage (95). Another day, lying naked on the same squalid bed, exposing herself to the sunlight that streams through the window when Rome is full of wild flowers in bloom, her body becomes a symbol of the city, with the Tiber river flowing into her pubic region, her body splendid as the flowers, and the hills curved toward her in sex waves (96-97). The door of her room has been left open, however, to the desiring eyes of her uncle, who lives with them in their miserable apartment. Sonia experiences moments of terror and shame the night her uncle rapes her during her sleep, after which the incestuous relationship— unnoticed by her vacuous mother even though it unfolds under her eyes—becomes a horrible, vulgar, lascivious hunt by the master for the servant.

After her uncle's departure from their household, a bitter and resentful Sonia, filled with a sense of horror and nausea, sees her mother as ugly, with arthritic hands, a face devastated by time, in a dirty, stained dress—a deformed personage, made up as a martyr, fashioning a stage on which Sonia is forced to play her role of a girl leading a subnormal life (112).

The flashback scene in which her hated father, the cavalry officer, during one of his rare visits to Marianna and Sonia, tries to force Sonia into marriage by using figurative whips and chains, is wholly dramatic. At her father's threat of withdrawal of all financial support, Sonia takes up the gauntlet from this nameless man who is ironically referred to throughout the book as "*il bell'ufficiale*" or simply "*il padre*," shouting out to him: "*Alla mamma ci penso io!*" (*I'll* take care of my mother! [125]). She has won her cause, both by refusing to marry[29] and by forcing her father to recognize his own cruelty and insensitivity towards Marianna. Now Sonia projects herself into a future "*da gigante*"—and it is interesting to note how often the words "*ingigantire*" (to magnify, exaggerate) and "*ingigantirsi*" (to grow gigantic) appear in her dreams and recollection images. Having been providentially locked in her room by her father for her insolence, the "gigantized" Sonia feels elated and "goes to sleep better to dream" (127).

During this earlier period of the flashback, Sonia felt deep tenderness for her defenseless, humiliated, and abased mother, whom she feels belongs to her and not to her father. She is maternal and protective towards Marianna, but their love is exasperated by loneliness, fear, and poverty. All of the daughter's earnings are dissipated by the totally irresponsible Marianna, who neither understands nor collaborates with Sonia. Unable to change her childhood habits, Marianna continues to live light-heartedly and frivolously in the happiness and remoteness of the past—a past that Sonia loves to dream about but at the same time must destroy in order to force her mother to face reality. From this conflictual situation there develops an understanding on Sonia's part of her father's desertion and cruelty, and a love-hate relationship with her mother, whom she is almost driven to strangle in her sleep. The dramatic scene in which both mother and daughter are on the verge of insanity out of sheer desperation takes the shape of a stunning symbol: the mother crouched on the floor in the position of a newborn child, with Sonia, in the throes of dizziness and disgust, hovering over her.

Having reached the limits of her physical and moral tolerance, Sonia finally decides that in order to change their life style, she must sacrifice herself by entering into a loveless marriage. Her choice falls on a silent, detached, hostile man, to whom she bears a son who grows up unhappily in the unnatural atmosphere of the household. Now, however, Sonia and her mother are elegantly dressed, well groomed, and enjoy the comfort of her husband's apartment—only for four months, however, because Marianna is stricken with breast cancer, and Sonia, deserted by her husband, in the process of nursing her dying mother, is completely transferred into her psychologically. At

Marianna's death, Sonia begins "accumulating remorse as others accumulate diabolic riches." The process unfolds like a literary panorama, without volume or weight, in which remorse is portrayed in timeless, superimposed, overlapping images, episodes, and apparitions, leading like so many labyrinthine paths out of Sonia's subconscious. She accuses herself of having been, paradoxically, the "sole person responsible for [Marianna's] life and for her death" (228). A month before her mother's demise, she had felt constrained to write a page because she "wanted to understand what she felt," and her writing permitted her the distance necessary for self-analysis, just as in Alba de Céspedes's *Forbidden Notebook*.

As the whole cast of characters ply in and out of Sonia's mind, growing larger and smaller, closer and then apart, the reader is caught up in the play of Sanvitale's film technique. The author skillfully depicts gigantic men in Sonia's life who seem to merge as they fly off her thoughts in a centrifugal movement, moving further and further away, getting smaller and finally disappearing. The story zigzags in time in an episodic, non-sequential style; it is not a succession of thoughts but of episodes that open out like pathways in simultaneous apparitions. The author frames events and feelings in cinematographic arrangements, prompting readers to follow the day-by-day happenings as though they were unwinding on a reel, and when the images slip off the reel, they become "gigantic."

The end of the novel brings us back, however, to the miniscule images of the beginning of the book, ready to disappear now that they have conveyed their message: Marianna and Sonia, throughout their entire lives, have stood immobile at the entrance to real life, staring at silent space to be filled, like two shipwrecked persons waiting, motionless, cautiously listening on a deserted beach, beyond which looms the forest (81). The cruelty of Marianna's lover, who is Sonia's father, in rejecting his beloved and refusing to recognize his illegitimate daughter, had contributed to creating an indissoluble bond of solidarity between the two women. Only now can the reader understand Sonia's deep love for her mother, her remorse at having scolded, threatened, and insulted her, and her regret at having failed to make her into an "imperial lady," satisfying her every whim. The story tells something one prefers usually not to discuss: that not only is it possible to love one's mother, but that it is impossible not to love her. The true value of the book, according to one critic,[30] lies in its complete sincerity in describing the

mother-daughter, love-hate relationship, as well as the impossible symbiosis that forces two beings to depend on each other
when one is irremediably attached to the past and the other to
the present and future.

Although Sanvitale's novel relates society's rejection of
an unwed mother and her child, it is not typically a feminist
novel; although it reconstructs the child's relationship to her
parents, to her legitimate and illegitimate relatives, and to
poverty as well, it is not typically a sociological novel; and despite the scenes of a young woman's social protests (e.g. that she
will never marry, yet finally does so, with all the consequent
traumas an unhappy marriage implies), *Madre e figlia* is not a
dramatic or a scenic novel, which would necessarily imply a restriction of the time and space dimensions.

There is a primordial sentiment of love-hate between
Sonia and Marianna, but there is also an eternal complicity between them, and herein perhaps lies the key for the interpretation of the last dream in which the pilgrim Sonia, together with
her son, finds herself in a beautiful foreign city. From her vantage point, on the left lies a wasteland devastated by war; on the
right, beyond the valley, an old paralyzed lady—the Queen—sits
immobile in a carriage. A cortege of old people mounted on
white horses stands motionless under an incessant rain, staring
fixedly, against a backdrop of a long wall of golden rock. The
impression gained is that for millenia nature and life had been
drawing this picture. Suddenly the entire scene changes into a
royal palace, as though men had come to realize what they can
do, together, given time: they can sculpture rock into a palace in
a kingdom to which old people can finally return to live happily.

Madre e figlia takes the reader through the young
heroine's psychological and archetypal evolution: the child at
first lives within a paradisical realm created by her mother in the
turn-of-the-century palace; her "fall" into life and the maturation process take place through encounters and struggles of
mythical proportions; and, in the end, a harmonious climate dif-
fuses the atmosphere as the old people are received into the
dream castle, a stupendous work achieved by humankind,
where Sonia's inner chaos is resolved. Her illusions are dis-
pelled, and her physical and spiritual maturity and integration
are finally wrought.

The discretion and delicacy with which Alba de Céspedes
and Francesca Sanvitale plead women's causes are matched by
the outspokenness and militancy of the aristocratically educated

Florentine, **Dacia Maraini** (1936-   ), daughter of Sicilian princess Topazia Alliata di Salaparuta and of Fosco Maraini, an oriental scholar. Maraini surprisingly turned out to be Italy's most
aggressive and prolific neofeminist theoretician, as well as an
outspoken bisexual who has always maintained that creativity is
linked to Eros and that the female body is material for novels
and poetry to be worked by women, and no longer by men.[31]
Deeply involved politically and widely traveled as a journalist,
Maraini, who is concerned about the problem of women's identity, is internationally known for her personal involvement in
the avant-garde on behalf of women's rights. Denouncing and
unmasking the oppression of her sex, hers is certainly one of the
most interesting, authoritative, and vociferously sustained
voices on the contemporary literary scene. Author of numerous
plays, essays, and short stories, as well as of three volumes of poetry, Maraini's novels include *La vacanza* (*The Holiday*, 1962),
which relates in a sensational style bordering on pornography
those sordid realities capable of producing existential nausea in a
fourteen-year-old girl; *Donna in guerra* (*Woman at War*, 1975), a
feminist ideological novel with sociological, political, and erotic
overtones, whose strong language and symbolic characters reveal the influence of the writer whose companion she had been
for eighteen years;[32] *Lettere a Marina* (Letters to Marina, 1981), a
confessional and more mature treatment of lesbianism than had
earlier and more polemically been presented in *Woman at War*;
Isolina: La donna tagliata a pezzi (Isolina: the woman cut into
pieces, 1985), a story based on actual fact of a cover-up trial in
Verona involving the killing of a young girl and the dissecting
of her body in order to save the honor of the nation's army and
the career of a single officer. In her novel, *La lunga vita di
Marianna Ucrìa* (The long life of Marianna Ucrìa, 1990, winner
of the Campiello Prize), Maraini evokes with anger and
tenderness the life of a deaf-mute woman in eighteenth-century
Sicily (see Chapter Two, above).

   L'età del malessere (*The Age of Malaise*, 1963, also translated as *The Age of Discontent*) is one of Maraini's most significant novels and the one that obtained the Prix Formentor as well
as international notoriety for the author. Again, Maraini draws
an emblematic portrait of a young girl-object pitilessly used by
others. The author speaks out with anger and force, as though
the girl's sordid existence were her own.

   The seventeen-year-old Enrica, who lives in one of the
poor sections of Rome, is left to herself by a distracted father and

an invariably tired and irritable mother. The incognizant and unfeeling Enrica acts unwittingly and experiences only brief sensations—of heat, cold, boredom, or brief pleasure when she makes love to Cesare, a boy from a "good family" who does not love her but merely uses her physical presence to interrupt the tedium of his studies. In the same spirit of carelessness and heedlessness with which she surrenders herself to Cesare, Enrica also obliges another schoolmate and a well-established lawyer. Finally, there surges in her the will to try a different life style. The final image of the protagonist is that of a transformed Enrica, determined to set out on a purposeful search for her autonomy, armed with full awareness of her worth as a woman.

Maraini's novels of introspection and psychological analysis go beyond the battle for women's emancipation and the myth of work as their best chance for liberation. She aims directly for sweeping changes in the entire politico-economic foundation of contemporary society, and, like so many of her coneofeminists, she demands for women the right to be protagonists in the historical process from which they have heretofore been excluded.[33] Yet, with respect to literature and style, Maraini makes no distinction between male and female: "There is but one style, there is but.one culture," she claims, adding that only the point of view changes—which is what makes for significant and substantial diversity. For whereas women writers do not moralize, men write about sex as sinful and almost always attribute the transgression to women.[34]

Chapter Seven

Journalists, Debutants of the Late 20th Century, and Other Professional Women as Authors of Novels

Among women who are prominent in their various professions (principally journalism and politics), there are some who have produced books and novels worthy of mention. First, however, a word should be said about the highly literary character of journalism in Italy. The snap grasp of a news event is no easy task for a newspaper reader, who first must undertake a preliminary burrowing through descriptions of baroque buildings with their frescoed or crumbling facades, or of hibiscus trees in bloom in a jittery city perhaps under a stage of siege. Writing for publication in a newspaper in Italy is not simply a reporting of facts but also an opportunity for the journalist to express personal views and reveal his or her talent in describing local color. The Italian journalist prefers him/herself as a creative artist, so the writer of style is constantly at loggerheads with the journalist whose duty is telegraphic reportage.

The colorful nineteenth-century journalist and poet, **Contessa Lara** (pseudonym of Eva Giovanna Antonietta Cattermole [1849-1896]), is the author of a novel, *L'innamorata* (The sweetheart, 1892), which gives the reader a sharp taste of bourgeois Rome during the era of King Humbert I.

Oriana Fallaci (1930-   ) is the unorthodox journalist, essayist, and novelist, notorious for her shameless and aggressive interviews that have been linked to boxing matches or love scenes. Some of her novels are as nonconforming as is her journalism: *Lettera a un bambino mai nato* (*Letter to an Unborn Child*, 1975), for example, created some scandal in Italy when it was first published since this dialogue between a solitary "emancipated" woman and her unborn child was nothing less than a political discourse on abortion, family, money, and the woman-lover relationship. Her 1990 novel, *Insciallah*, characterized as "a modern Iliad," offers exciting firsthand clarification of the entanglements of the Lebanese war even while magnifying the perversions of Italian males stationed in Beirut.

Fallaci's best-known novel, however, is the heartrending biography of her lover, the poet and Greek resistance hero Alexander Panagoulis, who was assassinated for political reasons in 1976: *Un uomo* (*A Man*, 1979). Fallaci herself describes the novel as a book on the solitude of the individual who refuses to be pigeonholed; a book on the tragedy of the poet who neither wishes to be, nor can ever be, a man of the masses and an instrument of those who command; and, finally, a book about a hero who fought alone for truth and freedom, and who died for refusing to surrender to government suppression and the acquiescence of the masses. Panagoulis has been assigned by History to the ranks of hero and political anarchist, but Fallaci has given him a higher title—that of a man—which in its utter simplicity, and in association with the intimacy that Fallaci brings to bear on the public and private figure, has brought the tormented Greek hero into the hearts of millions of readers. His vainglorious gestures and the needless risks he ran, betrayals by his companions and the torture he endured, have been indelibly impressed on the minds of those who have read Fallaci's novel. The living portrait drawn by the woman who shared an anguishing love affair with Panagoulis is one of the most extraordinary examples of the historical and inner biography of a man ever written by a woman.[1] The author succeeds in capturing the poignancy of their love affair and the pathos of the hero's drama in a piece of writing that soars far above her own journalistic métier.

Less bruising than Fallaci but equally abrasive with the subjects of her interviews is the politically and civically involved journalist **Camilla Cederna** (1911-   ). She tackles Italy's problems as well as the manners and customs of the bourgeoisie with doses of malice, venom, irony, and wit. Author of fifteen books, including an autobiography, *Il mondo di Camilla* (Camilla's world, 1980), her *Giovanni Leone, la carriera di un presidente* (Giovanni Leone, the career of a president, 1978) earned her a lawsuit and a sentence to pay damages to the family of a former president of Italy. Her target of attack in the 1988 volume entitled *De Gustibus* is the "neo-vulgar" behavior and misbehavior of Italian nouveaux-riches, while her presentation of about two hundred letters written by women to Mussolini during his twenty years of fascist government (*Caro Duce*, Dear Duce, 1989) contains the "heartening revelation" that the Duce was more at hand for many Italian women than their own husbands. He was the mythical figure who was present at their difficult moments. To him they related the frictions of daily life, to him they addressed their lamentations, and to him they protested the injustices of their working conditions.[2]

Leftist political scientist, journalist, feminist critic, and member of the European Parliament, **Maria Antonietta Macciocchi** (1922-   ) likewise analyzes the complex relationship between women and the fascist regime in *La donna "nera"* (The "black" woman, 1976) and *Le donne e i loro padroni* (Women and their masters, 1980) which aroused lively debate among exponents of the feminist movement in Italy. The singularly relevant work entitled *Dalla Cina* (1971, translated as *Daily Life in Revolutionary China*) remains one of the best written documents on that country's cultural revolution. The names of **Anna Del Bo Boffino**, **Miriam Mafai**, **Ida Magli**, **Rossanna Rossanda**, and **Carla Voltolina** must also be mentioned in the context of women professionals in the fields of sociology, psychology, feminist history, and cultural anthropology.

Fausta Cialente, the journalist whose *Le quattro ragazze Wieselberger* has already been considered (see Chapter Four, above), worked at the British General Headquarters in Cairo, Egypt, producing antifascist propaganda during World War II, and is the author of several novels that gained the attention of critics throughout her life: *Natalia* (1930), censored by the fascist government because it contains an episode of lesbianism; *Cortile a Cleopatra* (Courtyard to Cleopatra, 1936), the tragedy of a young boy who, after losing his father in Italy, returns to Egypt in search of his mother; *Pamela o la bella estate* (Pamela, or the fine summer, 1936), a story of adultery in a sensual Levantine setting; and *Ballata levantina* (*The Levantines*, 1961), a grandmother-granddaughter story set in Alexandria against a historical background of colonial conflict and two world wars. *Un inverno freddissimo* (A freezing winter, 1966), relating the realities of postwar Milan, focuses on a dismembered family painfully pieced together by a woman struggling against moral desolation and icy temperatures, while *Il vento sulla sabbia* (The wind on the sand, 1972) brings the reader back to the warmer climes of a mythical prewar Egypt, to which Cialente pays tribute in a somewhat bitter and detached final memoir.

Four journalists who have each written a novel are **Grazia Livi** (*L'approdo invisibile*, Invisible landing, 1981), whose Viareggio Prize-winning *Le lettere del mio nome* (The letters of my name, 1991) in the essay genre offers a stunning kaleidoscope of women who have shaped the author's intellectual growth; **Laura Lilli**[3] (*Zeta o le zie*, Zeta or the aunts, 1980); **Gabriella Guidi Gambino** (*Ti scrivo per confessarti*, I'm writing to confess, 1989); and **Lucia Annunziata** (*Bassa intensità*, Low intensity, 1990), a novel about guerrilla warfare in Salvador which reads like a reportage.

Maria Corti, author of philological and critical studies as well as the volume of short stories *Il canto delle sirene* that attracted the attention of several literary-prize juries and won the Ennio Flaiano International Prize in 1989, has also produced three novels, *Il ballo dei sapienti* (The dance of the wise, 1966); *L'ora di tutti* (Everyone's hour, 1962), a historical novel about an ineffable love which has benefited from an excellent analysis by Paola Blelloch;[4] and *Cantare nel buio* (Singing in the dark, 1991, winner of the Dessì literary prize), an epic about Italy's postwar Lombard workers which takes on symbolic value.

Of Piemontese origin, **Susanna Agnelli** was born in Turin in 1922 into the famous Fiat family. A political figure and activist in exhorting women to participate vigorously in public life, she militates for the Italian Republican Party, and has herself served as mayor of the town of Monte Argentario, member of the Chamber of Deputies of the Italian government, and member of the European Parliament. Agnelli's additional interests in journalism and narrative have resulted in the production of four books: *Vestivamo alla marinara* (We always wore sailor suits, 1975), her personal recollections of her childhood years and of World War II, related in a very matter-of-fact tone and with considerable name-dropping; *Gente alla deriva* (People drifting, 1980) about the arbitrary displacement of people of Vietnam, Laos, and Cambodia; *Ricordati Gualeguaychù* (see Chapter Five, above); and *Addio, addio mio ultimo amore* (Farewell, farewell my last love, 1985), in which she reveals why she is renouncing politics and the mayorship of Monte Argentario.

Two writers by the name of Ravera—Camilla and Lidia—unrelated to one another, deserve mention in this volume for disparate reasons. They belong to completely different generations, and write in dissimilar style for dissimilar purposes. Both Raveras converge as leftist militants who question in their works the place of women in Italian society.

Friend of Sibilla Aleramo (see Chapter Six, above), and Rome correspondent for Palmiro Togliatti, the versatile **Camilla Ravera** (1889-1988), who died aged ninety-nine, was a heroine of the Italian Communist Party, having filled the difficult role of party secretary and having served tirelessly in the antifascist struggle during much of her long life. Her 1937 novel, *Una donna sola* (A lonely woman), set in the region of Lucania in the 1930s, was published only as recently as 1988, winning the coveted Rapallo prize of that year, while her *Breve storia del movimento femminile in Italia* (Brief history of the feminist movement in Italy) received the Viareggio Prize in 1978.

Lidia Ravera (1951-   ), coauthor of the 1976 novel *Porci con le ali* (Pigs with wings) that was originally confiscated by the Italian Solicitor's Office as pornographic, but then became a bestseller among all age groups, outspokenly treats the phenomenon of Italy's sex revolution through the correspondence and sexual fantasies of two adolescent characters. Considered a lesser masterpiece of militant literature, the novel became, for Italy's leftist and restless youth, a vade mecum written in obsessively repetitious obscene language but containing the fears and hopes of an entire generation. *Per funghi* (Mushroom picking, 1987) relates the behavior of a group of forty-year-old men and women observed by an attentive, disenchanted Polly Anna, child of the 1968 revolution (Ravera's own generation), through whom the author expresses her pessimism with regard to the moral impoverishment of Italy's convoluted youth.

A success-scandal similar to that of *Porci con le ali* is the first narrative production, and now a film, *Volevo i pantaloni* (I wanted pants, 1989), of the nineteen-year-old Sicilian student **Lara Cardella**. A short, simple story—in which pants symbolize the desire for freedom—the book relates the cruelty of existence for young people of the author's age in a retrograde province of Italy. After Cardella, the youngest debutant on the literary scene is twenty-two-year-old **Silvia Ballestra**, another spokesperson for frustrated Italian youth in her *Compleanno dell'iguana* (The iguana's birthday, 1991).

Rarely do male literary critics bother to bring obscure women authors into the limelight. Pietro Citati is an exception, notably in his sensitive review of **Marta Morazzoni's** *Casa materna* (Maternal home, 1992). One of the niceties of established women writers is their supportiveness of lesser known novelists or debutants whose voices should be heard, if only to rescue them from the deaf ears of conceited "official" critics. Author **Giuliana Morandini** (*Da te lontano*, 1989; *Sogno a Herrenberg*, 1991) has focused some much needed attention on the figure of **Leda Rafanelli** (1880-1971),[5] a social, anarchical, "angry" writer of the early twentieth century who wrote, in addition to innumerable political tracts, the novels *Incantesimo* (Spell, written in 1919, published in 1921), and *L'oasi* (The oasis, 1929).

Natalia Ginzburg publicly proclaimed the ability of thirty-four-year-old **Susanna Tamaro** to capture the suffering of the weak and the defenseless in her *Per voce sola* (Voice solo, 1991), a book of five stories which have fascinated Federico Fellini as well. Surpassing other finalists, including **Serena Foglia** for her *I nostri sette peccati* (Our seven sins), Tamaro won the Pen Club Italiano and the Capri prizes for 1991.

The young **Clara Sereni** has received recognition by writers **Angela Bianchini** and **Adele Cambria** for her strange, self-recounting "recipe" novel entitled *Casalinghitudine* (Householditude, 1987).[6] Sereni was among the finalists for the 1989 Strega Prize for her volume of short stories, *Manicomio primavera*, taking the lead over **Paola Capriolo's** *Il nocchiero* which was, however, among the finalists for the Viareggio and the Campiello prizes for that year. Capriolo's most recent novel is *Il doppio regno* (Double reign, 1991).

Cambria has also cited **Elena Belotti's** *Fiore dell'ibisco* (Hibiscus flower, 1985) as the only feminist book that has made inroads on women's fiction; and she sees a fresh approach to the relationship of the couple in *Piazza, mia bella piazza* (My square, beautiful square, 1978)[7] by the now well-known writer, **Francesca Duranti**. Mention must be made of Duranti's *La casa sul lago della luna* (The house on the lake of the moon), which won the Bagutta and other prizes in 1984; her most recent novel, *Ultima stesura* (Final draft, 1991); and *Effetti personali* (1989 Campiello Prize). Considered her intensest and most mature novel, *Effetti personali* proceeds at a spy-story pace to narrate the adventurous journey, to an inaccessible Eastern European town, of a thirty-year-old divorcée (whose life seems to have lost its props, i.e. its "personal effects"), in a vain attempt to interview a famous writer. Essentially an illustration of two generations of feminists (a militant mother and a more mollified daughter), *Effetti personali* nicely weaves the theme of East-West perceptions, through the eyes of two young people in love, with considerations on aims and values in the literary world.

The name of **Vittoria Alliata** (*Harem*, 1980) is connected with women as travelers, while *Case di randagia* (Stray houses,

1989) relates the vagabond existence of the perennial traveler, **Colette Rosselli.**

Grazia Lago, besides poetry, has a novel to her credit—*Le vergini folli* (The foolish virgins, 1988), which earned the author characterization as a mannerist in the style of Italo Calvino.

The first novel of **Bianca Maria Frabotta,** author of *La letteratura al femminile* (Literature in the feminine, 1981), is an imaginary autobiography entitled *Velocità di fuga* (Flight speed, 1989). The work has been praised by writers Elisabetta Rasy and Francesca Sanvitale for its portrayal of a contradictory and only half-accepted creature in her tormented search for an elusive identity.

The name of **Gaia de Beaumont** is connected with *Venditore d'inchiostro* (The ink seller, 1983), which makes a mockery of love myths and male projections, as well as with *Bella* (The beauty, 1985), about "food and sex, sex and food."[8] **Francesca de Carolis's** first novel, *I giochi della Cometa* (Comet games, 1987) has been praised for the author's skill in handling dramatically and symbolically the appearance of Halley's comet in the skies of Rome in 1456, while **Romana Petri**'s novel, *Il ritratto del disarmo* (Portrait of dismantlement, 1991) is nicely filigreed with adaptations of the *Chanson de Roland.* **Luce D'Eramo,** a courageous woman author of French origin, set out in 1944 in search of the truth about German concentration camps. Remaining paralyzed in both legs as the victim of a bombing, she nonetheless returned to Italy to complete her university studies, and has come to be recognized not only as an author of novels on Nazi prison camps and terrorism, but also as Italy's sole woman author of science fiction. Journalist **Edith Bruck,** of Hungarian origin but writing in the language of the country of her adoption after deportation with her Jewish family, is the author of an autobiography, *Chi ti ama così* (Who loves you this way, 1959) that has been translated into five languages. She also wrote other novels on the theme of the solitary woman lost somewhere between the worlds of childhood and myth.

Involved in neither journalistic, nor literary, political, or sociological upheavals, the woman who has so distinguished herself in the field of science as to merit the 1986 Nobel Prize of Medicine,[9] **Rita Levi Montalcini (1909-   ),** has produced a book summing up the story of her studies, her heart, and her reasons:[10] *Elogio dell'imperfezione* (1987). Her autobiography, written in an impeccable narrative style, presents Levi Montalcini as a freethinker, staunch defender of human rights, and a brilliant researcher. *Elogio dell'imperfezione* unfolds in Italy, the United States of America, and South America, where, with horrific descriptions of cadaver dissections at medical school and caverns haunted by vampires and a strange Chilean neurophysiologist, Levi Montalcini follows Ariadne's thread into the mysterious labyrinth of the nervous system. Her volume is filled with imagery, humor, and irony, as she closely describes the world of science, World War II in her native Turin, and the Italian anti-Semitic laws of the fascist period. She also recalls the "family sayings" of the Levi Montalcini family and its sensitive position as Jews in a Catholic society.

An outstanding child at school, Rita especially loved Selma Lagerlöf's writings, Emily Brontë's *Wuthering Heights*, and Virginia Woolf's *To the Lighthouse*. Her relationship with her father, an engineer who raised his children to be free-thinkers like himself, was strained and uncommunicative. In writing *Elogio dell'imperfezione*, however, she recognizes her debt to him for the genes he transmitted to her. She admired his strength of character but resented the way his authority excluded her mother from having any say in family matters. Like Gianna Manzini in *Ritratto in piedi*, Levi Montalcini, through her book, tries to reconcile the father and daughter who mutually hurt one another.

In a chapter felicitously entitled "The weight of two X chromosomes in a Victorian atmosphere," she accurately evokes the frustration of women in the nineteenth century and the first decades of the twentieth, she herself having faced almost insurmountable barriers in attempting to enter higher institutions of learning. Victorian influence still being strong in matters of the raising of children, elementary schools were divided according to sex, sex determined the role waiting a child, and it was taken for granted that girls would become housewives, good wives, and mothers. Having rejected from adolescence the idea of creating a family, she decided to study medicine and, with her father's permission, entered the University of Torino, where her years of study in the early 1930s are fully described in the context of Italy's fascism.

After the outbreak of World War II, thwarted in her attempts to practice her profession, she renounced this intention and set up instead a laboratory in her own home to study the structure and function of the nervous system in chick embryos. Her scientific perseverance is tempered by fitting literary evocations throughout the autobiography: as she peers at the embryos through her microscope for what she is seeking she is reminded, for example, of Matilde Serao's description of Naples's populace on the feast of San Gennaro, pressing for the miracle of the liquefaction of the Saint's blood (156).

During the last years of the war, she was assigned to medical service in a war refugee camp, where the horrors she saw caused her to ponder, many years later, how her group of scientists could dedicate themselves with such enthusiasm to the analysis of a small problem of neuroembryology while Germans were ravaging Western civilization. She found her answer in the unconscious will to shut out what was happening around them because full awareness would have deprived them of the urge to live.

After the war, in 1947, she was invited to the United States to carry out research on the plasticity and ductility of the nervous system. Struck by the informality of the American educational system, she found particularly antipathetic the practice of women students' knitting during lessons—an activity that served to emphasize unduly the disparity of the sexes. She also sensed the frustration of some of the University professors' wives, who never realized their own careers and suffered overtly or covertly from the sense of their own moral nullity.

Having identified the proteinaceous substance able to stimulate nerve fiber growth (called NGF, nerve growth factor)—a discovery of fundamental theoretic importance because it paved the way to the discovery of other active growth factors in various types of cells[11]—Levi Montalcini, in the presence of the King of Sweden, graciously stepped aside to allow her charming personification of NGF to bow in acceptance of the Nobel Prize (216).

At the end of *Elogio dell'imperfezione*, Levi Montalcini traces, in six stunning pages (218-23), the evolution of the human brain from the time of Lucy, three-and-a-half million years ago, up to the modern era. Convinced that it is not innate ferocity nor aggressive instinct that has produced the horrors of the twentieth century but rather successful imprinting in the human brain by fanatic instigators and cynical leaders, she forces the reader to contemplate some of the hard choices humankind must make in order to free itself from dangerous propaganda. She, with her scientific skill, and her artistic twin sister, Paola, both lived their lives in a conscious movement towards a higher ideal. Their unwillingness to marry and their lack of maternal spirit facilitated their dedication to their activities; nor did they regret their choices. The example of the two sisters may be put forward for the young to follow. Through dedication to creativity and study as implements of knowledge rather than as bases for competition or as instruments of power, the human race can improve and elevate itself, refining its goals, and tempering its tools of art, science, and language in order to enhance its phylogeny.

This volume dedicated to Italian women authors who have striven to correct humanity's moral imperfection concludes with the portrait of Rita Levi Montalcini, who sensitively combines feelings for family and friendship with firmness in her dedication to science. Her autobiography is a sort of "final report" of her own personal efforts to move herself and the rest of humanity towards higher goals. Yet she fully recognizes the "imperfection" of that humanity. Perhaps she is the best example of the possibility of channeling feminine energies toward obtaining prizes of distinction, and of reaching the "crown" of Teilhard de Chardin's noosphere—a crown that might be placed, figuratively, on Levi Montalcini's own distinguished gray head.

Chapter Eight

Conclusion

The foregoing chapters have focused briefly on a century of Italian women prose writers. Undoubtedly, male authors have inspired, dominated, judged, or otherwise conditioned their female counterparts, but many Italian women writers have succeeded, on their own, in firming their reputation and communicating their personal messages. Giosuè Carducci gave needed encouragement to Annie Vivanti; Benedetto Croce was not reticent in evaluating (sometimes unfairly) his female literary contemporaries; Leonardo Sciascia claimed to have "discovered" Maria Messina; and Alberto Moravia exerted pertinaceous influence on Elsa Morante, Dacia Maraini, and his second wife, the budding novelist Carmen Llera. But the ongoing presence on the Italian literary scene of so many women authors (whose ranks are swollen by a large number of poets) bears witness to their contribution to the cultural heritage of their country and the making of its society.

Women authors have given literary expression to the injustices endured by Italian women whose accession to political, economic, and social parity with the male was achieved only as late as the mid-twentieth century. Some writers have concerned themselves with the incongruities, within the confines of a single nation, of an emancipated, industrialized, flourishing North divided from and looming over a depressed, backward South. (Still today a large segment of the South's female population persists in maintaining the status quo by traditional churchgoing, continuous and mindless bearing, and then raising, of children, often singlehanded in the absence of emigrant husbands; or by perpetuating the phenomenon of hazardous, clandestine abortions, even while their counterparts in the North have free access and attach no stigma to the essentially riskless operation.)

Other writers have stressed the effects of their country's turbulent history on families, of which women are considered the "pillars"; while still others have revealed their personal frustrations in a nation accustomed to assigning women to the realm of "householditude." (Statistics taken in 1989 reveal that only thirty per cent of Italy's women are gainfully employed, as compared with fifty-five per cent of the male population. The system of child care facilities is hopelessly inadequate. Very recent statistics indicate, however, that the aggregate Italian female population has the lowest fertility rate in the world, and that working women are making rapid strides in breaking away from the condition of householditude). An increasing number of qualified women are entering those professions heretofore restricted to males—military and police duties, the piloting of airplanes, and astronautics—even as more and more sensitive and resourceful Italian women are becoming successful explorers of the "immense continent" that is literature.

Modern woman, in the view of Cardinal Giacomo Biffi as expressed in a homily from the pulpit of St. Peter's Church in Bologna on the feast of the Immaculate Conception in 1989, is anathema and "*squallida*" (dismal, inconsequential, worthy of disesteem). Italian women of the ilk of Rita Levi Montalcini and Dacia Maraini have publicly responded to the Cardinal. Those Italian women who have broadly widened their sphere of intellectual activity and made their mark as writers and thinkers in both Italy and abroad speak for themselves.

The impetus for the continuing forward movement of women writers and philosophers is all the more remarkable in such a complex and contradictory nation as Italy, where institutions and social structures change rapidly, but capriciously and inconsistently. Women are bringing a greater consistency to bear, however, as they repeatedly challenge the dictum that if Sappho takes a husband, *he* goes to his writing table, *she* to the kitchen.

Notes

Preface

[1] See Chapter Seven, below.

[2] Pierre Teilhard de Chardin, *Le phénomène humain* (Paris: Editions du Seuil, 1955), 180.

[3] Elsa Morante, "Nove domande sul romanzo," cited in Gianni Venturi, *Morante*, Il Castoro 130 (Firenze: La Nuova Italia, October 1977), 1.

[4] Mario Miccinesi, *Deledda*, Il Castoro 105 (Firenze: La Nuova Italia, September 1975), 6.

[5] Cf. Maria Rosa Cutrufelli, ed., *Scritture, scrittrici* (Milano: Coop Longanesi & C., 1988), 18, 20.

Chapter One

[1] Elsa Morante repeatedly sustained that the distinction between "*scrittori*" and "*scrittrici*" smacked of racism—as though cultural categories were a function of biological distinctions—and she deemed the separate generic concept of "women writers" as characteristic of a harem society.

[2] Interview by Paolo Tortonese, *Corriere della Sera*, 24 January 1988.

[3] See Chapter Three, note 4, below.

[4] Neria De Giovanni, *L'ora di Lilith. Su Grazia Deledda e la letteratura femminile del secondo Novecento* (Roma: Ellemme, 1987), 72-74.

[5] Women authors of this period have been neatly divided into generations by the contemporary writer, Giuliana Morandini, in her introduction to *La voce che è in lei. Antologia della narrativa femminile tra '800 e '900* (Milano: Bompiani, 1980), 8, 9: the generation born between 1800-1820 remained succubus to masculine models, often used masculine or exotic pseudonyms, and sometimes dissociated themselves from feminism, going so far as to repudiate their womanhood. Women writers born between 1820-1840, in treating the problems of life during the risorgimento, gave a social tint to their writings and found publishers for their works more easily than their predecessors. The generation born between 1840-1860 was stymied by the political and economic crises of the 1880s and 1890s. The era of positivism having brought with it repressive, limiting feminine stereotypes, women writers, thrown off their course, reverted to "escapist" literature of the early twentieth century, writing "sentimental"

novels and children's books. The generation born between 1860-1880 was more organized, had more weight on the literary scene, and formed literary associations as in England. Recognition of women increased, for it was in 1861 that the first proposal to grant women the vote was made, even though over eighty years were required for legal recognition of this right, in 1945. (After that date, however, in forty years' time, Italian women have rapidly achieved juridic equality in almost all fields. See Chronology, above. Author's note.) The generation born between 1880-1890, when women's activities and initiatives were differentiated from those of males, when pseudonyms were still fashionable but at least were female names, saw the exploration of feminine existence and recognized in it a wealth of unexploited dramatic specificity. From the turn of the century on, literary feminism developed nicely in Anglo-Saxon countries and in France, but in the countries moving towards dictatorial regimes (Italy and Germany) there was a hiatus. It was not until the resistance movement and the end of World War II that the development continued in Italy.

[6] Italian *verismo* originated in French realism and naturalism, and was represented in Italy during the late nineteenth and early twentieth centuries by Verga, Deledda, Luigi Capuana, the early D'Annunzio, and Matilde Serao, *inter alios*.

[7] Translated by Rosalind Delmar (Los Angeles: University of California Press, 1980); also translated as *A Woman at Bay* by Maria H. Lansdale (New York and London: Putnam, 1908).

[8] Neria De Giovanni (*L'ora di Lilith*, 109) points out that the elite circles of the literary avant-garde in the early 1960s were often extreme leftist ideologically.

[9] Immediately following World War II, feminine groups linked to political parties usually served a purely organizational (and not ideological) purpose. They formed a chain of information for the ideology of the party made up of men, studied by men, who then decided on the problems of women. Just the opposite occurred in the 1970s: women separated themselves from men in a minirevolution apart from the evolution of the Italian political line of the day. This separation brought together women across different social strata—a positive effect—but the feminist movement was not susceptible to dialectical evolution and became an "ism" like all others, empty of meaning, without embracing women's problems as part of all other problems (cf. *Riflessi degli squilibri socio-economici e dell'attuale crisi sulla condizione femminile a livello comunitario e nazionale*, Proceedings of International Women's Year Convention, 1975, 26-27, passim). As suggested in the preface of the present work, the movement of women's efforts cannot be separated from the general flow of history, progress, and evolution.

[10] An indication of how deeply rooted among Italians is reverence for maternity is the government's stance on protecting pregnant women workers: inordinately long leaves-of-absence with pay (two months prior to delivery and up to nine moths postpartum leave) are so generous that some employers balk at the outset at hiring women. Motherhood, the argument goes, is extremely important for the health of society and future generations. Meanwhile, however, as recounted by Susanna Agnelli (see Chapter Seven, below), the library of the town where she served as mayor remained closed for two years because the librarian (a highly protected position substantially preclud-

ing the hiring of temporary help) had two children in succession—a situation that helps perpetuate the pitifully low statistics on Italy's reading habits.

[11] For a more recent model of emancipation as demystification of sexual taboos, see Anna Nozzoli's *Tabù e coscienza* (Firenze: La Nuova Italia, 1978).

[12] Cf. also Gianna Manzini's *Lettera all'editore*, Chapter Five, below.

[13] Patricia M. Spacks, *Imagining a Self* (Cambridge: Harvard University Press, 1976), 18.

[14] Abridged translation by Adrienne Foulke, New York: Harcourt, 1951.

[15] Francesca Sanvitale, "Novecento. Letteratura italiana dal 45 ad oggi," RAI Uno, 15 November 1989. A word may perhaps be said here about the general inadequacy of Italian television in providing literary programs for its viewers. Particularly notorious is the twenty-minute weekly program "Novecento," which supposedly is dedicated to Italian books published since 1945. Apart from the startling fact that the bookshelves that serve as backdrop are garnished with much meaningless paraphernalia but pitifully few books, the subjects of discussion—ostensibly intended to recreate the atmosphere of the literary period involved—are mainly political, economic, and social, with large segments of documentary reels showing such figures as presidents, popes, Frank Sinatra, Elvis Presley, and Marilyn Monroe. A literary Italian television program of the seriousness of the French "Apostrophes" and "Caractères" is probably unrealistic for Italy, whose television viewers, it is thought, must be entertained rather than instructed.

[16] See also Carol Lazzaro-Weis, "Gender and Genre in Italian Feminist Literature in the Seventies," *Italica* 65 (1988), 293-307.

[17] Enzo Golino, "L'Italia analfabeta," *La Repubblica*, 9 September 1988, 10.

Chapter Two

[1] Grazia Deledda, *Premio Nobel per la letteratura 1926* (Milano: Fabbri, 1966), 22.

[2] See also Chapter Four, below.

[3] From Philip Revzin in *The Wall Street Journal*, 21 November 1988.

[4] As an antidote to the horrors of Naples described in *Il ventre di Napoli*, the reader would be well advised to plunge into the dreams and fantasies of the highly lyrical short stories contained in Serao's *Leggende napolitane* (Neapolitan legends, 1881), in which she mythologizes and personifies in magical style the pleasant localities and famous islands of Naples.

[5] Ironically, Ortese, one of Italy's finest writers and winner of no fewer than four literary prizes, lives in almost dire poverty, blind and alone except for a group of friends and admirers who have obtained for her a government stipend under the Italian "Bacchelli law" which provides financial help for distinguished Italians in need.

[6] Cf. Anna Nozzoli's introduction to *Il mare non bagna Napoli* (Firenze: La Nuova Italia, 1979), IX-XVI.

[7] The island has been celebrated also by Alphonse de Lamartine in his autobiographical novel, *Graziella* (1852).

[8] Gianni Venturi, *Morante*, Il Castoro 130 (Firenze: La Nuova Italia, October 1977), 78.

[9] Maria Messina, *La casa nel vicolo* (Palermo: Sellerio, 1982), 17-43, passim.

[10] Cf. especially Elsa Morante's *History: A Novel, House of Liars*, and *Aracoeli*.

[11] Giuseppe Tedeschi, "Intervista con Livia De Stefani dopo 'La Signora di Cariddi,'" *Il Dramma* I (1972): 24.

[12] Cf. Elena Clementelli, "Livia De Stefani," *Letteratura Italiana. I Contemporanei* V (1974), 772-76.

[13] The theme of the death decree imposed on "sinners" by government authority and a delegated inquisitor underlies the apocalyptic *La stella Assenzio* (The star Wormwood, 1985), a novel in which Livia De Stefani pinpoints, in terms of the biblical Book of Revelation, the earth's contemporary drug and ecological scourges, and uncannily highlights, before the fact, the disaster of Chernobyl (the Ukrainian word "chernobyl" means wormwood). Cf. *Book of Revelation*, Chapter 8, verses 10-11 and *La stella Assenzio*, (Firenze: Vallecchi, 1985), 23-24, 96.

Chapter Three

[1] Regarding women's rhythmic and cyclical concept of time, measurable through her own physiological functions, see also Paola Blelloch, *Quel mondo dei guanti e delle stoffe* . . . (Verona: Essedue Edizioni, 1987), 152-53.

[2] Neria De Giovanni, *L'ora di Lilith*, 117.

[3] Giorgio Torelli, "Maria Bellonci: un drink coi Borgia," *Epoca*, 4 March 1973, 53.

[4] Bellonci's *Lucrezia Borgia* so caught the fancy of Simon Harcourt-Smith that he plagiarized it in *The Marriage at Ferrara* (London: John Murray, 1953), resulting in the withdrawal of the volume from circulation by the publisher. Women novelists, it may be noted here, remain remarkably guiltless of unauthorized copying of other authors' works.

[5] *Confessioni di scrittori. (Interviste con se stessi). Quaderni della Radio XI*, 1951, 20.

[6] Torelli, "Maria Bellonci," 54. Not all historical figures, however, lend themselves to Bellonci's involuntary autobiographies. She has stated that Marie Antoinette and Napoleon the General, for example, do not enter the scope of her poetic world, but that Napoleon at St. Helena would, because there he becomes an expression of the human condition of suffering and reaction to it through moral strength. *Ibid.*

[7] Banti is the author of biographies of Matilde Serao (1965), with whom she has been compared, of Fra Angelico (1953), Lorenzo Lotto (1953), Diego Velasquez (1955), and Claude Monet (1956).

[8] Cf. Blelloch, *Quel mondo*, 156.

[9] G. A. Peritore, "Anna Banti," *Letteratura Italiana. I Contemporanei* III (1969), 215.

[10] Cited by John Wakeman, ed., *World Authors, 1950-70* (New York: H. W. Wilson Co., 1975), 113-14.

[11] Loy's first novel, *La bicicletta* (Viareggio Prize, 1974) and her 1982 novel, *L'estate di Letuchè*, are presently enjoying a revival on bestseller lists.

[12] One of the few works whose translation into Japanese has been subsidized by the Italian government.

[13] *La vie: mode d'emploi* (Paris: Hachette, 1978, quoted in *La Repubblica*, 30 December 1988).

[14] *Contemporary Literary Criticism* (Detroit, Michigan: Gale Research Company, 1978), 404.

[15] Published in 1968, long before the late Philippe Soupault's *Poésies pour mes amis les enfants* (1983), in which Soupault expresses his joy at being understood by children. A comparative study of these two surrealist authors would be a welcome contribution to the literature.

[16] For a psychoanalytic analysis of the characters of Anna and Concettina, see Bettina Knapp, *Women in Twentieth-Century Literature: A Jungian View* (University Park and London: The Pennsylvania State University Press, 1987), 69-85.

[17] The novel has been seen as a study of the impact of a historical situation on two social classes: the young intellectual bourgeoisie of the fascist and post-fascist eras, and the landworkers, who were incapable of playing any significant role in the nation's political history. Cf. Luciana Marchionne Picchione, *Natalia Ginzburg*, Il Castoro 137 (Firenze: La Nuova Italia, September 1975), 42-43.

Chapter Four

[1] Marisa Rusconi, "Nuovi percorsi tra esperienza e scrittura," in Cutrufelli, *Scritture, scrittrici*, 15.

[2] De Giovanni, *L'ora di Lilith*, 48.

[3] Rusconi, "Nuovi percorsi," 18.

[4] One good illustration is the novel, *Conclusione* (1901), by the jealous, antifeminist yet battered wife (Teresa, using the pseudonym, Calista) of Edmondo De Amicis, author of the famous children's book, *Cuore* (1884). Cf. *La Repubblica*, 4 August 1989, 20.

[5] For an analysis of Deledda's creative imagination as eros, with its connected sacred rituals, see De Giovanni, *L'ora di Lilith*, 23-50.

[6] Negri's birthplace, Lodi (near Milan) is the seat of the "Ada Negri" Poetry Prize awarded each year to the author of an unpublished poem.

[7] *Dadapolis*, edited by Fabrizia Ramondino and Andreas F. Müller (Torino: Einaudi, 1989).

[8] Cf. Rosanna Fiocchetto, "Il viaggio," in Cutrufelli, *Scritture, scrittrici*, 49.

[9] Rusconi, "Nuovi percorsi," 12-13.

[10] A nice complement to Cialente's work is Giuliana Morandini's *Da te lontano* (Trieste: Dedolibri, 1989), an anthology of documents connected with Triestine culture from the eighteenth to the twentieth century.

[11] Alcide Paolini, Preface to *Le quattro ragazze Wieselberger* (Milano: Mondadori, 1976), IX.

[12] Fiora Vincenti, "Lalla Romano," in *Letteratura Italiana. I Contemporanei IV* (1974), 649.

[13] Fiora Vincenti, *Lalla Romano*, II Castoro 94 (Firenze: La Nuova Italia, October 1974), 2, 5. Further illustration of Romano's excessive autobi-

ographism may be found in her published books of family album photographs that are the subject of an article by Flavia Brizio, "The Photographic Novels of Lalla Romano," American Association for Italian Studies at the University of Lowell, 9th Annual Conference, 13-16 April 1989.

[14] Giorgetti's earlier work, a collection of short stories entitled *Il giocatore del silenzio* (Player of silence), was concomitantly awarded the 1954 Viareggio Prize and rejected by a New York publisher as too much of a risk. Cf. *American postuma*, 165.

[15] Quoted by Piero De Tommaso, "Natalia Ginzburg," *Letteratura Italiana. I Contemporanei* III (1969), 824.

[16] Cf. Maria Bellonci (Chapter Three, above, p. 41).

[17] Cited in Enzo Panareo, *Invito alla lettura di Gianna Manzini* (Milano: Mursia, 1977), 116.

[18] *Ibid*, 111.

[19] Cf. Abraham, Giorgio and Peregrini, Claudia, *Ammalarsi fa bene* (Milano: Feltrinelli, 1989). In the autobiography of Thomas Bernhard, the author sustains that only during "hospitalization"—real or figurative—does one's thinking process take on vital and decisive importance for one's existence.

[20] See Elena Gianini Belotti, "I volti di lui," in Cutrufelli, *Scritture, scrittrici*, 57-59.

[21] Cf. Jean Noël Schifano, "Barbara e divina," *L'Espresso*, 2 December 1984, 128. Dostéyevsky similarly had imagined and fully described, in *The Diary of a Writer*, the circumstances of a real criminal trial before they were actually revealed.

[22] Where Elsa Morante's ashes are interred, unless accusations leveled in 1988 against her friend, stage director Carlo Cecchi, prove to be valid. Cecchi, in compliance with the author's dying wish, allegedly opened the tomb, stole Morante's ashes, and sprinkled them over the sea around the island of Procida.

[23] John Wakeman, ed., *World Authors 1950-70*, 1025.

[24] It will be recalled that Morante's father was a native of Sicily.

[25] Venturi, *Morante*, 35.

[26] For an analysis of Elisa's reading as pleasurable mystification or disruptive questioning, see Valeria Finucci, "The Textualization of a Female "I": Elsa Morante's *Menzogna e sortilegio*," *Italica* 65 (1988), 308-9.

[27] "Una sera un libro," RAI television broadcast of 29 June 1989.

Chapter Five

[1] Umberto Eco, "Tre donne intorno al cor . . . ," *Carolina Invernizio. Matilde Serao. Liala*, Il Castoro 145 (Firenze: La Nuova Italia, January 1979), 7.

[2] Neera, *Una passione* (Milano, Palermo, Napoli: Remo Sandron, n.d.): 98, 99.

[3] For an analysis of writing as a cognitive undertaking in the so-called "Epistolario" of *House of Liars*, see Finucci, "Textualization," 314-22.

[4] Cf. Pietro Frassica, "Gina Lagorio and Tosca's Solitude," *Italica* 65 (1988), 338.

[5] Bellonci's character was undoubtedly inspired by the figure of Reginald Pole (1500-1558), an English cardinal who, on several occasions, almost be-

came pope but in the end was tried for heresy. Six letters in the Vatican archives written by Marchesa Vittoria Colonna (1490-1547) to Reginald Pole, and probably known to Bellonci, have recently been published under the title "Nuovi documenti su Vittoria Colonna e Reginald Pole," *Collectanea archivi vaticani*, N. 24.

Chapter Six

[1] Liala, *Tutto Libri*, 8 July 1978, cited by Maria Pia Pozzato in "Liala," Umberto Eco et al., *Invernizio*, 98.

[2] As reported by Anna Banti, cited by Isabella Pezzini in "Matilde Serao," *ibid.*, 64.

[3] Pozzato, "Liala," 117-18.

[4] Marina Federzoni, "Carolina Invernizio," *ibid.*, 48-49.

[5] Umberto Eco, "Tre donne intorno al cor . . . ," *ibid.*, 25.

[6] Federzoni, "Carolina Invernizio," 46.

[7] Morandini, *La voce che è in lei*, 16.

[8] Natalia Ginzburg, who wrote a stunning autobiographical introduction to the 1973 edition of Colombi's *Un matrimonio in provincia* (Torino: Einaudi), mentions in *Family Sayings* (see Chapter Four, above) that her mother thought highly of Marchesa Colombi's writings and regretted the difficulty of finding editions of her works (213)—as does this author.

[9] Nozzoli, *Tabù*, 5.

[10] Fiora A. Bassanese, *"Una donna*: Autobiography as Exemplary Text," *Quaderni d'italianistica* XI, 1 (1990): 44.

[11] The semi-autobiographical *Zingaresca* (1917), containing descriptions of Vivanti as mother and writer, was studied by Anne Urbancic in "L'Io-narrante autobiografico di Annie Vivanti," American Association for Italian Studies at the University of Lowell, 9th Annual Conference, 13-16 April 1989.

[12] Cf. Nozzoli, *Tabù*, 11-16.

[13] G. A. Borgese, "Un romanzo di Annie Vivanti," *La vita e il libro* III (1913): 234.

[14] Nozzoli, *Tabù*, 15.

[15] Cf. Ferdinando Castello, "La vita non è recita ma ricerca," *La Civiltà Cattolica*, 3 May 1980, 366-71.

[16] Cutrufelli, *Scritture, scrittrici*, 71-72.

[17] See Chapter Five, above.

[18] *Confessioni di scrittori. (Interviste con se stessi)* (Torino: Edizioni Radio Italiana, 1981), 9.

[19] Bassanese, *"Una donna*," 43.

[20] Nozzoli, *Tabù*, 39-40.

[21] Quoted in Bassanese, *"Una donna*," 53.

[22] Elisabetta Rasy, *Le donne e la letteratura: scrittrici eroine e ispiratrici nel mondo delle lettere* (Roma: Editori Riuniti, 1984), 127.

[23] By Isabel Quigly, (London: Harvill Press, 1957 and New York: Simon and Schuster, 1958) but throughout I have retained the more literal translation of the title in order to preserve the figurative and personifying intention of the author.

24 Maria Assunta Parsani and Neria De Giovanni, *Femminile a confronto—Tre realità della narrativa italiana contemporanea: Alba de Céspedes, Fausta Cialente, Gianna Manzini* (Manduria: Lacaita, 1984), 36.

25 Nozzoli, *Tabù*, 152.

26 *Ibid.*, 153 ff.

27 *Ibid.*, 155.

28 For an extended analysis of this novel, see Fiora A. Bassanese, "Armanda Giuducci's Disposable Women," in Santo L. Aricò, ed., *Contemporary Women Writers in Italy. A Modern Renaissance* (Amherst: The University of Massachusetts Press, 1990), 153-69.

29 Cf. Article 13 of the Declaration of Mexico City in Proceedings of International Women's Year Convention, 1975: "The respect of human dignity includes the right of every woman to decide freely and personally whether she will marry or not." One positive aspect of marriage for women in Italy is that they never surrender their maiden names, which remain attached to their juridical person. No form of "Ms" exists in Italian, prevailing usage being to address as "Signora" any woman who is apparently over eighteen years of age. This writer would like to propose—as the equivalent of Ms—"Signa," a reduction of both "Signora" and "Signorina."

30 Blelloch, *Quel mondo*, 106-7.

31 Female eroticism is the subject of the first issue (1990) of a new Italian women's magazine, *Tuttestorie*, directed by Maria Rosa Cutrufelli and edited by Marisa Rusconi.

32 Maraini has always recognized her debt to Alberto Moravia; she admires his intellectual honesty, his understanding, and his concern for social problems. Despite their separation, they were bound by friendship and mutual esteem. In a 1981 interview, Maraini stated that she owed much to Moravia even though she now worked only for herself and for women. Cf. Carla Stampa, "Scrivo inebriandomi con il basilico," *Epoca*, 2 May 1981, 121.

33 Nozzoli, *Tabù*, 150.

34 Stampa, "Scrivo inebriandomi," 123.

Chapter Seven

1 Cf. Blelloch, *Quel mondo*, 75.

2 *La Repubblica*, 9 March 1989, 32.

3 Lilli must also be credited with having brought to public attention the works of Paola Masino (1908-89), author of an unusual novel with feminist overtones, *Nascita e morte della massaia* (1945). Cf. *La Repubblica*, 28 July 1989.

4 Blelloch, *Quel mondo*, 76-80. Blelloch has also given attention (71-72) to Carla Cerati, one of the finalists for the Comisso Prize in 1990 for her novel, *La cattiva figlia*.

5 Morandini, *La voce che è in lei*, 21, 284-307, 376-81, 395-96.

6 Cutrufelli, *Scritture, scrittrici*, 34-36, 39-40.

7 *Ibid.*, 41.

8 *Ibid.*, 64-65.

9 Shared with American biochemist Stanley Cohen, who clarified the structure of the substance (NGF) identified by Levi Montalcini.

10 For a study of the problematic relationship between women and science from ancient times up to the first half of the nineteenth century, see Margaret Alic's *L'eredità di Ipazia.   Donne nella storia della scienza dall'antichità all'Ottocento* (Roma: Editori Riuniti, 1989).

11 At the time of this writing, Levi Montalcini was pondering a revolutionary hypothesis: that NGF, besides stimulating nerve fiber growth, has many other vital functions in the human organism including, perhaps, the stimulation of the mind itself. *La Repubblica*, 13 July 1989, 18.

Selected Bibliography

Primary Sources

Adorno, Luisa. *Arco di luminara*. Palermo: Sellerio, 1990.

Agnelli, Susanna. *Addio, addio mio ultimo amore*. Milano: Mondadori, 1985.

—. *Gente alla deriva*. Milano: Rizzoli, 1980.

—. *Ricordati Gualeguaychù*. Milano: Club del libro, 1982.

—. *Vestivamo alla marinara*. Milano: Mondadori, 1975.

Aleramo, Sibilla. *Una donna*. Roma-Torino: Soc. Tip. Ed. Naz., 1906.

Banti, Anna. *Artemisia*. Milano: Mondadori, 1953. (Gli Oscar, 1974).

—. *La camicia bruciata*. Milano: Mondadori, 1973.

—. *Noi credevamo*. Milano: Mondadori, 1967.

—. *Un grido lacerante*. Milano: Rizzoli, 1981.

Bellonci, Maria. *Lucrezia Borgia*. Milano: Mondadori, 1939.

—. *Rinascimento privato*. Milano: Mondadori, 1985.

—. *Segreti dei Gonzaga*. Milano: Mondadori, 1947.

—. *Tu vipera gentile*. Milano: Mondadori, 1972.

Bossi Fedrigotti, Isabella. *Di buona famiglia*. Milano: Longanesi, 1991.

Cardella, Lara. *Volevo i pantaloni*. Milano: Mondadori, 1989.

Cederna, Camilla, ed. *Caro Duce*. Milano: Rizzoli, 1989.

—. *De gustibus*. Milano: Mondadori, 1986.

—. *Giovanni Leone, la carriera di un presidente*. Milano: Feltrinelli, 1978.

—. *Il mondo di Camilla*. Milano: Feltrinelli, 1980.

Chiomenti Vassalli, Donata. *Donna Olimpia, o Del nepotismo nel Seicento*. Milano: Mursia, 1979.

—. *I fratelli Verri*. Milano: Ceschina, 1960.

—. *Giovanna d'Aragona*. Milano: Mursia, 1986.

—. *Giulia Beccaria, la madre del Manzoni*. Milano: Ceschina, 1956.

Cialente, Fausta. *Le quattro ragazze Wieselberger*. With a preface by Alcide Paolini. Milano: Mondadori, 1976.

Colombi, Marchesa. *In risaia*. Milano: Treves, 1878.

—. *Un matrimonio in provincia*. Milano: Treves, 1878.

—. *Un matrimonio in provincia*. With an introduction by Natalia Ginzburg. Torino: Einaudi, 1973.

Corti, Maria. *L'ora di tutti*. Milano: Feltrinelli, 1977.

de Céspedes, Alba. *Nessuno torna indietro*. Milano: Mondadori, 1938.

—. *Prima e dopo*. Milano: Mondadori, 1955.

—. *Quaderno proibito*. Milano: Mondadori, 1952. (Gli Oscar, 1967).

Deledda, Grazia. *Le opere: Il vecchio della montagna. Elias Portolu. Cenere. Canne al vento.* Milano: Edizione speciale CDE su Licenza della Arnoldo Mondadori Editore, 1955.

—. *Premio Nobel per la Letteratura 1926.* Milano: Fratelli Fabbri, 1966. (Volume contains unpublished letters of Deledda and Swedish Academy discourse.)

—. *Romanzi e Novelle.* Vols. III, IV. Milano: Mondadori, 1950, 1955.

De Stefani, Livia. *La stella Assenzio.* Firenze: Vallecchi, 1985.

—. *La vigna delle uve nere.* Milano: Mondadori, 1953.

Di Falco, Laura. *L'inferriata.* Milano: Rizzoli, 1976.

Drigo, Paola. *Maria Zef.* Milano: Treves, 1936.

—. *Maria Zef.* Translated and with an introduction by Blossom Steinberg Kirschenbaum. Lincoln and London: University of Nebraska Press, 1989.

Duranti, Francesca. *Effetti personali.* Milano: Rizzoli, 1989.

Fallaci, Oriana. *Il sesso inutile: Viaggio intorno alla donna.* Milano: Rizzoli, 1961.

—. *Insciallah.* Milano: Rizzoli, 1990.

—. *Lettera a un bambino mai nato.* Milano: Rizzoli, 1975.

—. *Niente e così sia.* Milano: Rizzoli, 1969.

—. *Penelope alla guerra.* Milano: Rizzoli, 1962.

—. *Se il sole muore.* Milano: Rizzoli, 1965.

—. *Un uomo.* Milano: Rizzoli, 1979.

Ferri, Giuliana. *Un quarto di donna.* Venezia: Marsilio, 1973.

Frigeri, Mariana. *Il condottiero. Vita, avventure e battaglie di Bartolomeo Colleoni.* Milano: Longanesi, 1985.

—. *Ludovico il Moro. Un gentiluomo in nero.* Milano: Editoriale nuova, 1980.

Ginzburg, Natalia. *All Our Yesterdays.* Translated by Angus Davidson. Exeter, England: Carcanet Press, 1985.

—. *Caro Michele.* Milano: Mondadori, 1973.

—. *La città e la casa.* Torino: Einaudi, 1984.

—. *La famiglia Manzoni.* Torino: Einaudi, 1983.

—. *Le piccole virtù.* Torino: Einaudi, 1966.

—. *Lessico famigliare.* Torino: Einaudi, 1963.

—. *Le voci della sera.* Torino: Einaudi, 1961.

Giorgetti, Silvana. *America postuma.* Roma: Carte segrete, 1972.

Guiducci, Armanda. *Donna e serva.* Milano: Rizzoli, 1983.

—. *Due donne da buttare.* Milano: Rizzoli, 1976.

—. *La donna non è gente.* Milano: Rizzoli, 1977.

—. *La mela e il serpente.* Milano: Rizzoli, 1974.

Jaeggy, Fleur. *I beati anni del castigo.* Milano: Adelphi, 1989.

Jarre, Marina. *I padri lontani.* Torino: Einaudi, 1987.

Lagorio, Gina. *Approssimato per difetto.* Bologna: Cappelli, 1971.

—. *Fuori scena.* Milano: Garzanti, 1979.

—. *Golfo del Paradiso.* Milano: Garzanti, 1987.

—. *Tosca dei gatti.* Milano: Garzanti, 1983.

—. *Tra le mura stellate.* Milano: Mondadori, 1991.

—. *Un ciclone chiamato Titti.* Bologna: Cappelli, 1969.

Levi Montalcini, Rita. *Elogio dell'imperfezione.* Milano: Garzanti, 1987.

Livi, Grazia. *Le lettere del mio nome.* Milano: La Tartaruga, 1991.

Loy, Rosetta. *Le strade di polvere.* Torino: Einaudi, 1987.

Manzini, Gianna. *La sparviera.* Milano: Mondadori, 1956.

—. *Lettera all'editore*. Firenze: Sansoni, 1945.

—. *Ritratto in piedi*. Milano: Mondadori, 1971.

—. *Sulla soglia*. Milano: Mondadori, 1973.

Maraini, Dacia. *Donna in guerra*. Torino: Einaudi, 1975.

—. *Isolina. La donna tagliata in pezzi*. Milano: Mondadori, 1985.

—. *La lunga vita di Marianna Ucrìa*. Milano: Rizzoli, 1990.

—. *La vacanza*. Milano: Lerici, 1962.

—. *L'età del malessere*. Torino: Einaudi, 1963.

—. *Lettere a Marina*. Milano: Bompiani, 1973.

Messina, Maria. *La casa nel vicolo*. Milano: Treves, 1921. Palermo: Sellerio, 1982.

Morandini, Giuliana. *Da te lontano*. Trieste: Dedolibri, 1989.

Morante, Elsa. *Aracoeli*. Torino: Einaudi, 1982.

—. *Diario 1938*. Torino: Einaudi, 1989.

—. *Il mondo salvato dai ragazzini*. Torino: Einaudi, 1971.

—. *La Storia*. Torino: Einaudi, 1974.

—. *L'isola di Arturo*. Torino: Einaudi, 1957.

—. *Menzogna e sortilegio*. Torino: Einaudi, 1948. (Prima edizione negli "Struzzi," 1975).

Neera. *L'indomani*. Palermo: Sellerio, 1981.

—. *Una passione*. Milano, Palermo, Napoli: Remo Sandron, n.d.

Negri, Ada. *Stella mattutina*. Milano: Mondadori, 1921.

Ortese, Anna Maria. "Dieci domande ad Anna Maria Ortese." *Nuovi argomenti* 51-52 (1976): 5-11.

—. *Il mare non bagna Napoli*. Firenze: Vallecchi, 1967. (Edited by Anna Nozzoli. Firenze: La Nuova Italia, 1979.)

—. *In sonno e in veglia*. Milano: Adelphi, 1987.

—. *L'iguana*. Firenze: Vallecchi, 1965.

—. *Poveri e semplici*. Firenze: Vallecchi, 1967.

Ramondino, Fabrizia. *Althénopis*. Torino: Einaudi, 1981.

—. *Dadopolis*. Edited by Fabrizia Ramondino and Andreas F. Müller. Torino: Einaudi, 1989.

—. *Taccuino tedesco*. Milano: La Tartaruga, 1987.

Ravera, Camilla. *Una donna sola*. Roma: Editrice Lucarini, 1988.

Ravera, Lidia. *Per funghi*. Roma: Theoria, 1987.

—. *Porci con le ali*. With Marco Lombardo Radice. Roma: Savelli, 1976.

Romano, Lalla. *La penombra che abbiamo attraversato*. Torino: Einaudi, 1964.

—. *Le lune di Hvar*. Torino: Einaudi, 1991.

—. *Le parole tra noi leggere*. Torino: Einaudi, 1969.

—. *Nei mari estremi*. Milano: Mondadori, 1987.

—. *Una giovinezza inventata*. Torino: Einaudi, 1979.

—. *Un sogno del Nord*. Torino: Einaudi, 1989.

Sanvitale, Francesca. *Il cuore borghese*. Milano: Mondadori, 1986.

—. *Madre e figlia*. Torino: Einaudi, 1980.

Serao, Matilde. *Leggende napoletane*. Milano: Ottimo, 1881. (Napoli: Libreria Economica, 1907).

—. *Il paese di cuccagna*. Milano: Treves, 1891. (Milano: Treves, 1928).

—. *Il ventre di Napoli*. Milano: Treves, 1884. (Roma: Edizioni Vito Bianco, n.d. [1973?]).

—. *Vita e avventure di Riccardo Joanna*. Milano: Galli, 1887. (Milano: Garzanti, 1939).

Sereni, Clara. *Casalinghitudine*. Torino: Einaudi, 1987.
—. *Manicomio primavera*. Firenze: Giunti, 1989.
Sereni, Marina. *I giorni della nostra vita*. Roma: Edizioni di cultura sociale, 1955.
Vassalli, Donata Chiomenti. *Giovanna d'Aragona. Tra Baroni, Principi e Sovrani del Rinascimento*. Milano: Mursia, 1987.
Vivanti, Annie. *I divoratori*. Milano: Quintieri, 1911.
—. *Marion*. Milano: Mondadori, 1939. (Original version, Bergamo: Chiesa e Guindani, 1891).
—. *Naja Tripudians*. Milano: Mondadori, 1921.
—. *Vae victis!*. Milano: Rusconi, 1981.

Secondary Sources

Books:

Alic, Margaret. *L'eredità di Ipazia. Donne nella storia della scienza dall'antichità all'Otttocento*. Roma: Editori Riuniti, 1989.
Aricò, Santo L., ed. *Contemporary Women Writers in Italy. A Modern Renaissance*. Amherst: The University of Massachusetts Press, 1990.
Biagini, Enza. *Anna Banti*. Milano: Mursia, 1978.
Birnbaum, Lucia Chiavola. *Liberazione della donna: Feminism in Italy*. Middletown, Connecticut: Wesleyan University Press, 1986.
Blelloch, Paola. *Quel mondo dei guanti e delle stoffe. . . .* Verona: Essedue Edizioni, 1987.
Bosetti, Gilbert. *Le mythe de l'enfance dans le roman italien contemporain*. Grenoble: Ellug, 1987.
Bullock, Alan. *Natalia Ginzburg*. NY/Oxford: Berg Publishers Ltd., 1991.
Caccamo, Rita. *Il filo di Arianna*. Milano: Franco Angeli, 1987.
Carrano, Patrizia. *Le signore "grandi firme"*. Rimini-Firenze: Guaraldi, 1978.
Ceratto, Marina. *Il "Chi è" delle donne italiane, 1945-82*. Milano: Mondadori, 1982.
Confessioni di scrittori. (Interviste con se stessi). Quaderni della Radio XI. Torino: Edizioni Radio Italiana, 1951.
Contemporary Authors. Detroit, Michigan: Gale Research Company, annual.
Contemporary Literary Criticism. Detroit, Michigan: Gale Research Company, annual.
Costa-Zalessow, Natalia, ed. *Scrittrici italiane dal XIII al XX secolo. Testi e critica*. Ravenna: Longo, 1982.
Croce, Benedetto. *La letteratura della nuova Italia* (3). Bari: Laterza, 1964.
Cutrufelli, Maria Rosa, ed. *Scritture, scrittrici*. Milano: Coop Longanesi & C., 1988.
De Giovanni, Neria. *L'ora di Lilith. Su Grazia Deledda e la letteratura femminile del secondo Novecento*. Roma: Ellemme, 1987.
Eco, Umberto, Federzoni, Marina, Pezzini, Isabella, and Pozzato, Maria Pia. *Carolina Invernizio. Matilde Serao. Liala*. Il Castoro 145. Firenze: La Nuova Italia, 1979.
Gastaldi, Mario. *Dizionario delle scrittrici italiane contemporanee*. Milano: Gastaldi, 1957.

Grillandi, Massimo. *Invito alla lettura di Maria Bellonci*. Milano: Mursia, 1983.

Guzzetta, Lia Fava. *Manzini*. Il Castoro 96. Firenze: La Nuova Italia, 1974.

I riflessi degli squilibri socio-economici e dell'attuale crisi sulla condizione femminile a livello comunitario e nazionale. Proceedings of International Women's Year Convention, Rome, Italy, 10 July 1975.

Irigaray, Luce. *Io, tu, noi. Per una cultura della differenza*. Torino: Bollati Boringhieri, 1992.

Knapp, Bettina L. *Women in Twentieth Century Literature: A Jungian View*. University Park and London: The Pennsylvania State University Press, 1987.

Kunitz, Stanley J. and Haycraft, Howard. *Twentieth Century Authors*. New York: H.W. Wilson Co., 1942.

Letteratura italiana. I Contemporanei. Vols. III, IV, V. Milano: Marzorati, 1969, 1974.

Livi, Grazia. *Da una stanza all'altra*. Milano: Garzanti, 1984.

Lombardi, Olga. *Invito alla lettura di Grazia Deledda*. 2nd ed. Milano: Mursia, 1983.

Marchionne Picchione, Luciana. *Natalia Ginzburg*. Il Castoro 137. Firenze: La Nuova Italia, 1978.

Miccinesi, Mario. *Deledda*. Il Castoro 105. Firenze: La Nuova Italia, 1975.

Morandini, Giuliana. *La voce che è in lei. Antologia della narrativa femminile italiana tra '800 e '900*. Milano: Bompiani, 1980.

Nozzoli, Anna. *Tabù e coscienza*. Firenze: La Nuova Italia, 1978.

Panareo, Enzo. *Invito alla lettura di Gianna Manzini*. Milano: Mursia, 1977.

Parsani, Maria Assunta and De Giovanni, Neria. *Femminile a confronto—Tre realtà della narrativa italiana contemporanea: Alba de Céspedes, Fausta Cialente, Gianna Manzini*. Manduria: Lacaita, 1984.

Rasy, Elisabetta. *Le donne e la letteratura: scrittrici eroine e ispiratrici nel mondo delle lettere*. Roma: Editori Riuniti, 1984.

Sgorlon, Carlo. *Invito alla lettura di Elsa Morante*. 3rd. ed. Milano: Mursia, 1978.

Teilhard de Chardin, Pierre. *Le phénomène humain*. Paris: Editions du Seuil, 1955.

Venturi, Gianni. *Morante*. Il Castoro 130. Firenze: La Nuova Italia, 1977.

Vincenti, Fiora. *Lalla Romano*. Il Castoro 94. Firenze: La Nuova Italia, 1974.

Wakeman, John, ed. *World Authors, 1950-70*. New York: H.W. Wilson Co., 1975.

—. *World Authors, 1970-75*. New York: H.W. Wilson Co., 1980.

Articles:

Aricò, Santo L. "Oriana Fallaci's Journalistic Novel: *Niente e così sia*." *Contemporary Women Writers in Italy. A Modern Renaissance*. Amherst: The University of Massachusetts Press, 1990, 171-82.

Banti, Anna. "La Serao a Roma." *Paragone* 182/2 (1965): 37-55.

Bartolomei, Giangaetano. "Psicoanalisi di Carolina Invernizio." *Belfagor* 28 (1973): 109-15.

Bassanese, Fiora A. "Armanda Guiducci's Disposable Women." *Contemporary Women Writers in Italy. A Modern Renaissance.* Amherst: The University of Massachusetts Press, 1990, 153-69.

—. "*Una donna*: Autobiography as Exemplary Text." *Quaderni d'italianistica* XI, 1 (1990): 41-60.

Battaglia, Salvatore. "Le 'frantumate lontananze' di Gianna Manzini." *Il Dramma* 6 (1971): 101-106.

Bellesia, Giovanna. "Camilla Cederna: Portrayer of Italian Society." *Contemporary Women Writers in Italy. A Modern Renaissance.* Amherst: The University of Massachusetts Press, 1990, 185-96.

Blelloch, Paola. "Francesca Sanvitale's *Madre e figlia*: From Self-Reflection to Self-Invention." *Contemporary Women Writers in Italy. A Modern Renaissance.* Amherst: The University of Massachusetts Press, 1990, 125-37.

Borgese, G.A. "Un romanzo di Annie Vivanti." *La Vita e il libro* III (1913): 231-41.

Brizio, Flavia. "Memory and Time in Lalla Romano's Novels, *La penombra che abbiamo attraversato* and *Le parole tra noi leggere*." *Contemporary Women Writers in Italy. A Modern Renaissance.* Amherst: The University of Massachusetts Press, 1990, 63-75.

—. "The Photographic Novels of Lalla Romano." American Association for Italian Studies at the University of Lowell, 9th Annual Conference (13-16 April 1989).

Capozzi, Rocco. "Elsa Morante: The Trauma of Possessive Love and Disillusionment." *Contemporary Women Writers in Italy. A Modern Renaissance.* Amherst: The University of Massachusetts Press, 1990, 11-25.

Castelli, Ferdinando. "La vita non è recita ma ricerca." *La Civiltà Cattolica* 3117 (1980): 366-71.

Clementelli, Elena. "Livia De Stefani." *Letteratura Italiana. I Contemporanei* V (1974): 771-83.

Costa, Simona. "Ipotesi per un 'ritratto' di Gianna Manzini." *La Rassegna della letteratura italiana* 3 (1974): 467-79.

Del Greco Lobner, Corinna. "A Lexicon for Both Sexes: Natalia Ginzburg and the Family Saga." *Contemporary Women Writers in Italy. A Modern Renaissance.* Amherst: The University of Massachusetts Press, 1990, 27-42.

De Tommaso, Piero. "Natalia Ginzburg." *Letteratura Italiana. I Contemporanei* III (1969): 817-33.

Finucci, Valeria. "The Textualization of a Female 'I': Elsa Morante's *Menzogna e sortilegio*." *Italica* 65 (1988): 308-28.

Frassica, Pietro. "Gina Lagorio and Tosca's Solitude." *Italica* 65 (1988): 329-43.

Golino, Enzo. "L'Italia analfabeta." *La Repubblica*, 9 September 1988.

Groppali, Enrico. "Natalia Ginzburg." *Rivista Italiana di Drammaturgia* II, 6 (1977): 103-10.

Heller, Deborah. "History, Art, and Fiction in Anna Banti's *Artemisia*." *Contemporary Women Writers in Italy. A Modern Renaissance.* Amherst: The University of Massachusetts Press, 1990, 45-60.

Lazzaro-Weis, Carol M. "From Margins to Mainstream: Some Perspectives on Women and Literature in Italy in the 1980s." *Contemporary Women Writers in Italy. A Modern Renaissance.* Amherst: The University of Massachusetts Press, 1990, 197-217.

—. "Gender and Genre in Italian Feminist Literature in the Seventies." *Italica* 65 (1988): 293-307.

Malpezzi Price, Paola. "Autobiography, Art, and History in Fausta Cialente's Fiction." *Contemporary Women Writers in Italy. A Modern Renaissance.* Amherst: The University of Massachusetts Press, 1990, 109-22.

Miceli-Jeffries, Giovanna. "Gianna Manzini's Poetics of Verbal Visualization." *Contemporary Women Writers in Italy. A Modern Renaissance.* Amherst: The University of Massachusetts Press, 1990, 91-106.

Molesini, Andrea. "Una lettera di Luigi Pirandello a Neera." *Studi novecenteschi* 34 (1987): 209-15.

Peritore, G.A. "Anna Banti." *Letteratura Italiana. I Contemporanei* III (1969): 211-34.

Pietralunga, Mark F. "Gina Lagorio and the Courage of Women." *Contemporary Women Writers in Italy. A Modern Renaissance.* Amherst: The University of Massachusetts Press, 1990, 77-88.

Pischedda, Bruno. "Annie Vivanti." *Belfagor* 46 (1991): 45-64.

Pupino, Angelo R. "Elsa Morante." *Letteratura Italiana. I Contemporanei* III (1969): 715-43.

Scaramucci, Ines. "Anna Maria Ortese." *Letteratura Italiana. I Contemporanei* V (1974): 887-901.

Schifano, Jean Noël. "Barbara e divina." *L'Espresso*, 2 December 1984, 122-33.

Stampa, Carla. "Scrivo inebriandomi con il basilico." *Epoca*, 2 May 1981, 118-23.

Tamburri, Anthony J. "Dacia Maraini's *Donna in guerra*: Victory or Defeat?" *Contemporary Women Writers in Italy. A Modern Renaissance.* Amherst: The University of Massachusetts Press, 1990, 139-51.

Tedeschi, Giuseppe. "Intervista con Livia De Stefani dopo 'La signora di Cariddi.'" *Il Dramma* I (1972): 24-25.

Torelli, Giorgio. "Maria Bellonci: un drink coi Borgia." *Epoca*, 4 March 1973, 52-56.

Urbancic, Anne. "L'Io-narrante autobiografico di Annie Vivanti." American Association for Italian Studies at the University of Lowell, 9th Annual Conference (13-16 April 1989).

Vecchi, M. L. "Ritratti critici di contemporanei: Gina Lagorio." *Lettore di provincia* 65-66 (1986): 48-58.

Vincenti, Fiora. "Lalla Romano." *Letteratura Italiana. I Contemporanei* IV (1974): 639-55.

Zambon, Patrizia. "Maria Messina, *Piccoli gorghi*. Ada Negri, *La Cacciatora e altri raccolti*." *Studi novencenteschi* 17 (1990): 199-203.

Index